808.5

SPEECH COMMUNICATION

WILLIAM NORWOOD BRIGANCE

Late of Wabash College

SPEECH

COMMUNICATION

Second Edition

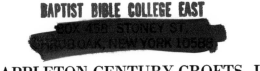
APPLETON-CENTURY-CROFTS, Inc.

New York

PREFACE

In 1941 Mr. F. S. Crofts asked whether I would undertake a "brief textbook" in speechmaking, one that presented the concepts of new trends then emerging. He did not use the word "communication," and in fact I don't think educators themselves then commonly used the word. But that was what he meant. I replied that it would depend on the kind of brief textbook he wanted. If he wanted a condensed, and hence necessarily abstract, treatment of the full body of principles, then I was not the one to do it. I was convinced that a condensed abstract treatment of the whole field could not help students, but could only confuse them. But if he wanted a brief textbook in which the author selected the minimum principles thought necessary, omitted the others, and treated this selected minimum fully and as vividly as possible, then I was willing.

We considered the hazards. Every teacher who might use the book would have his own opinion on which were the minimum principles to be put in, and which left out. They would differ with one another, and with the author. They would ask: "Why was so-and-so left out?" and "Why was such-and-such included?" Inevitably some would say, "Away with him! He has left out certain basic principles!"

In the end we decided to take the risk. The "brief textbook" would be brief because it included only the minimum essentials, treated fully and vividly, and left out others, however useful or helpful they might be. It was a risk, but a calculated risk, as all life is a calculated risk.

A war intervened, and the "brief textbook" did not appear until 1947. The reaction was more favorable than I had supposed. Most teachers accepted as a fact of life that no author's selection would coincide with theirs. Indeed, in general they approved the selection; and those who thought additional principles might be added were careful to emphasize that they would rather have the book as it was than to add or expand at the cost of increasing the size.

After six years, however, I was able to get the consensus of users

v

on changes they would like to have, and during the past two years I have revised the book accordingly. Those who used the first edition certainly did not agree on proposed changes in the revision. There were sharp differences of opinion. But the consensus in each case was by a large majority, in no case under 75 per cent. On the basis of this consensus I have established for the revision the following standards:

1. Not to increase the over-all length, but to reduce somewhat the space given to specimen speeches and to add that amount to the body of the text.

2. To add a preliminary chapter on Managing Ideas, always a critical problem for students, so as to give them maximum aid early in the course.

3. Not to expand the treatment of Action, Voice, and Group Discussion, but to recast certain details and if possible to improve them.

4. To expand the treatment of Outlining and spell out the principles in greater detail. As one colleague wrote, "Students are weak in outlining. They need all the help a textbook can possibly give them."

5. To expand the Forms of Supporting Materials.

6. To expand the treatment of Persuasion and give it emphasis by a separate chapter.

7. To add a chapter on Listening.

Perhaps I ought to dedicate this revision to the teachers who were kind enough to give me the benefit of their experience. Or perhaps it should be dedicated to the students who will benefit from the trial and error of those who have gone before.

Wabash College   W. N. B.

CONTENTS

ILLUSTRATIONS

SPEECH COMMUNICATION

Chapter 1

THE RIGHTS OF LISTENERS

At the turn of the twentieth century mass communication had five standard media: books, magazines, newspapers, the stage, and the public platform. During the twentieth century three new ones were developed, each of which carries the human voice around the world: the moving picture, radio, and television. These are the *eight physical media* of communication available to modern man. But man —even modern man—still has only *three basic forms* of communicating to others via these eight media. All three are old, very old. They are prose, poetry, and public address. You have already studied prose and poetry, its forms and its literature. Most of you have not studied public address at all, so let us start by examining its basic difference from prose and poetry.

Prose and poetry are composed by absentee authors, set down on paper, and received at a time and place that suits the reader's convenience. Not so with public address. To be sure, the speaker composes the material in absentia, but composing the material is only the essential preliminary. He must then create the speech by appearing in person and talking to living listeners. These listeners sit before him. They are visible to him—except on radio and television, where they are not visible physically but are sharply in his mind's eye and are listening at the moment of utterance. In creating the speech, the speaker talks *to* these listeners. He talks *with* them. He looks *at* them. He sees their nods of understanding or telltale expressions of misunderstanding, their attentive look which says "I am interested," or their bored restlessness which says "I am tired of listening." Public address, then, is not set down on paper for somebody to read next week or next month. It is spoken to people at the moment of utterance. Public address, then, not only requires previous composition of material. It also requires the speech to be *created on the instant and in the presence of the listeners.*

1

You hardly need to be told that to do this well requires skill and training. Indeed it requires so much skill and training that most books on the subject are compelled, for sheer lack of adequate space, to concentrate on the speaker entirely and to neglect the listener. So lest we fall into the same pitfall, we shall look first at the listener's problems, then after that at the speaker's.

In a proper sense, the listeners are more important than the speaker, even though the speaker has the more difficult role. They are more important because public address in a free society exists to serve listeners, not speakers. From the listeners' standpoint entirely too much public talk is trite, dull, boring, or simply worthless. Too much is perpetrated by self-made speakers who have never learned how to create a speech on the instant and in the presence of listeners. Some have never learned how to manage themselves in public. Some have not learned how to manage their ideas. Some have not learned either. Some believe that "anybody can talk," and demonstrate vengefully their false belief. Some have what Emerson described tartly as a selfish enjoyment of their sensations, "and loss of perception of the sufferings of the audience." Some really drone only to themselves, and never actually reach out and talk to the listeners. Some speak only in generalities, which, even if they glitter, create what Mark Twain described as "confusion of the mind and congestion of the ducts of thought." They may be summarized by Oliver Wendell Holmes' caricature in *The Autocrat of the Breakfast Table:* "Self-made men?—Well, yes. . . . It is a great deal better to be made in that way than not to be made at all."

There is no justifiable place for such speaking. There is a place only for speaking that is worth listening to; and *speaking is not worth listening to unless it delivers useful goods to the listener.* The two things, then, that every listener has a right to expect of a speaker are these:

1. *Useful* goods.
2. Ability to *deliver* these goods.

Let us consider them in detail and in more formal language.

From a Speaker, Listeners Have the Right to Expect Interesting and Useful Ideas

The typical educated person hears approximately one hundred speeches a year. Why listen to so many? Why listen to *any?* Not because we are forced outwardly, for outwardly we are free to listen or not. We are rather driven by forces within us. We are human beings, living in a very real world. In that world we face problems which in a free society must be understood by responsible people. We are beset by choices and temptations. We are haunted by shadows of fear. We listen to speakers, then, because we hope they will throw light on our problems, temptations, and fears. We listen because we hope they will give us new information, new ideas, or will simply water and cultivate old ideas. We listen because we want to be given encouragement, to renew our faith, to strengthen our determination. Or perhaps we listen because we want to escape from reality for a time, to laugh and forget our troubles.

These are the services expected of speakers, and listeners have the inalienable right to demand that every speaker who consumes public time shall deliver the services expected. The following three types of speakers, to state it bluntly, are parasites who do not deliver the expected goods and who ought to be put out of business:

1. *The Stratosphere Speaker*—who never gets down to earth where ordinary mortals live and breathe, but speaks from the stratosphere of abstract and hazy words. He seldom cites a fact; he never takes the trouble to illustrate thought by an illustration; he never relieves a tired audience by humor. He soars at high altitude where all is hazy and vague. Here is a verbatim quotation from such a specimen:

> We have learned in the past, and now it has been catastrophically reaffirmed, that this world is cosmos.

What did he mean? Oh, possibly that, "This is one world." One cannot be sure. The speaker probably was not too sure himself. The Stratosphere Speaker simply misses the purpose of public speaking. He thinks of it as an altitude flight, whereas *the purpose of public talk is to water and cultivate ideas on important subjects, and this requires plain words, plain facts, and specific ideas.*

2. *The Witless Wit*—who believes in the salvation of man by funny stories. He is determined to set the audience in a roar, and comes armed with twenty anecdotes—but no thought. He recites with gusto his hodgepodge of jests, which illustrate no theme, and measures his success by the amount of laughter. To listeners who have previously heard part or all of the jokes, they are no longer funny.

3. The Phonograph—who reproduces a magazine article and thinks it makes a good speech. The Phonograph is a common species among students. He is the one who puts off preparing a speech until the night before, then evades the issue by seizing a magazine article, swallowing it undigested, and attempting to reproduce it as a speech. He does not plagiarize outright; that is, he does not recite verbatim the words of the article. But he does reproduce the outline and the contents, and he adds nothing of his own. He is a Phonograph, and his speech is a failure, because even a good article when recited is not a speech. "The voice is Jacob's voice, but the hands are the hands of Esau." That magazine article was written six months or a year ago. It was written for perhaps a million readers, people of varied educational levels, scattered over the entire United States and in foreign lands. In contrast, the speech is to be given _today_ to one particular group of thirty people who have already heard two speeches on the same general topic during the past month, and it is given by a student whose voice and manner proclaim loudly that he knows nothing about the subject except what he is reciting from the magazine. In other words, the student has failed to focus the speech on the particular audience meeting at a particular place on a particular day. Being a Phonograph, he simply reproduces another person's thoughts.

Listeners Also Have the Right to See and Hear a Human Being Who Talks with the Audience, and Not a Dull or Nervous Creature Who Talks Mainly to Himself

There are unthinking people who believe that "delivery" is not important, that a speaker needs only to "say what he thinks" and these thoughts will somehow find their way into the minds of the audience. A fair statement of this belief is, "It does not matter how you deliver a speech; the only important thing is what you say." Now this is a comfortable belief. It relieves the speaker from any responsibility beyond writing a paper. But it is naive, unreal, and does not square with the facts of life. It assumes that you literally "deliver" a speech in the same way you deliver a loaf of bread. It assumes that when delivered, the speech, like the loaf of bread, arrives intact and cellophane-wrapped no matter how long the delivery man took, whether he arrived drunk or sober, or how many detours or breakdowns he had along the way. These are grand assumptions, but only assumptions, for _there is no such thing as delivering a_ *speech.* The very word "delivery" is a turn of expression and not a statement of fact.

WHY NO SPEAKER CAN REALLY "DELIVER" A SPEECH

You can deliver a book, a pencil, or a loaf of bread. You carry them to their destination and give them up to another's keeping. You cannot so deliver a speech. What we call delivering a speech is actually *translating a speech through seven stages from your mind to the mind of the listener. These seven stages are as follows:*

1. You start with a *thought* in your mind.

2. This thought is coded into a series of impulses and sent through your nervous system. These impulses are roughly like a dot-dash telegraph code, and are known as a *neurogram.*

3. This neurogram is coded further into phonetic symbols by *muscular movements* of the tongue, lips, face, diaphragm, etc.

4. These phonetic symbols, thus produced by muscular activity, are coded still further into *sound waves* that travel invisibly through the air. When these sound waves reach the listener, the decoding process begins.

5. The sound waves *strike the listener's ear drums* and produce a mechanical action in the bones of the middle ear and in the fluid of the inner ear. In this process the sound waves are decoded again into phonetic symbols.

6. These decoded phonetic symbols are sent in the form of impulses along the nerve fibers to the brain. These impulses, as in Stage 2, are roughly like a dot-dash telegraph code, and compose a *neurogram.*

7. In the listener's brain this neurogram is decoded further into a *thought.* This last step is the semantic stage, wherein the various brain assemblages translate the incoming symbols into meaning. The amount of meaning in each instance will depend on: (1) the distinctness and clarity of incoming symbols, and (2) the variety of brain connections, built-in and temporary, that are available for use.

Thus you do not "deliver" a speech at all in the way you deliver a book, a pencil, or a loaf of bread. There is no "delivery" to it. Instead you *use sound waves and light waves to create thought in the listener's mind.*

So far, of course, we have discussed only sound waves. This was not because light waves are not important or not inherent, but simply because the complex process loosely called "delivery" is more easily understood if taken one part at a time. We now can consider light waves. They follow a process parallel to that of sound waves: (1) The *thought* in the speaker's mind is coded into (2) a *neurogram* in the nervous system, then (3) further coded into *muscular movements* of posture, body, hands, face and head. These in turn are (4) transmitted by *light waves* that are (5) received by the listener's *eyes* where they are (6) decoded into a *neurogram* via nerve impulses sent along the optic nerve to the brain. Finally, in the brain this is (7) decoded into a *thought*. Now this thought is not so refined and exact as the thought conveyed by words, but it is older in the human race, is written deeper in the human organism, and carries more basic meanings. Sound waves carry the refined, precise thought. Light waves carry the broad basic background of meaning. To the listener they say, "That speaker does not mean what he says; his actions deny his words." Or, "He is not thinking, but only reciting." Or, "I see exactly what he means, for he both *shows* and *tells* me."

WHY SPEAKERS FAIL IN "DELIVERY"

The following are common types of speakers who create barriers that prevent their arousing full thought in listeners' minds:

1. *The Fidgeter*—whose actions distract the listeners' attention. The eye is quicker than the ear. What the listener sees takes priority over what he hears. Hence the Fidgeter's actions interfere with his words. Behold the Fidgeter's behavior: If his hands are in his pockets, he takes them out; if they are out, he puts them in. If his coat is unbuttoned, he buttons it; if it is buttoned, he unbuttons it. If he is at one side of the platform, he paces to the other side; when he gets there, he paces back again. He rocks from heel-to-toe. He stands on one foot, and hoists the other as though to cool off the sole of his shoe. His hands and feet are always in the way, and he has the air of having too many of them.

2. *The "And-Er" Vocalist*—whose pauses mutilate instead of punctuate. Instead of a clean pause at the end of a thought phrase, he creates static like this:

I—*Er* wonder if—*Er*—we might not want—*Er*—to look at the—*Er* ten most popular plays of the—*Er*—year.

To *Er* is human; but to listeners, it is exasperating, and in speakers it is unforgivable. They should be forced to listen to a recording of their voices.

3. *The Mumbler*—who can hear himself and does not care if others cannot. He looks at the ceiling, at the floor, or out the window, but not at the audience. He keeps his mouth closed "like the front room in an old-fashioned farmhouse," and opens it only to eat and yawn. His lips and tongue are on vacation. His jaw is fixed and rigid, like the much-pictured Rock of Gibraltar. His voice is flat, and his tones are weak. He believes that talk is cheap, and his talk is cheap indeed.

4. *The Listless Voice*—who talks loud enough to be heard, but who lacks vocal emphasis, inflection, and variety of tone. His words are without color, informing inflection, warmth, friendliness, or life. He simply drones in a listless voice. The result of this type of speaking was frankly stated by Edward R. Murrow in assessing former Prime Minister Clement R. Atlee's listless voice; his speaking was "not a success," because he managed to "discuss the whole subject as though elucidating some obscure unimportant passage in a Latin translation."

It may be self-satisfying to the speaker with a listless voice to imagine that how he talks does not matter, that what he says is the only thing that counts. But the plain truth is otherwise. Experimental evidence suggests that listeners will remember only about 40 per cent as much of what is spoken in a listless voice as compared with that spoken in a voice with lively emphasis, variety, and inflection. Imagine two speakers. Both talk loud enough for every word to be heard, but one speaks with color, warmth, and informing inflection; the other speaks in a tone that does not vary in pitch, time, intensity, or quality. The audience will remember only about 40 per cent as much of what is said by the listless speaker as compared with what is said by the lively speaker.

To summarize: *In speaking, the know-how as well as the know-what is important; and audiences have the right to demand that speakers face this fact honestly and frankly, that they take an inventory of their competence and overcome the barriers of fidgeting, of articulating "and-er's," of mumbling, and of speaking in a listless voice.*

CONVERSING WITH THE AUDIENCE

Basically, public speaking is enlarged conversation, and it should be enlarged enough to fill the room and reach that slightly hard-of-hearing listener in the eighth row who leans a little forward as you begin to talk. This requires certain mental, and perhaps moral, qualities that are well stated by James A. Winans as follows:

1. *Full realization of the content of your words as you utter them,* and

2. *A lively sense of communication*[1]

When the first element is lacking—that of fully realizing the content of words at the instance of utterance—the delivery is *absent-minded*. When the second element is lacking—the lack of a lively sense of communication—the speaker seems to be *talking to himself*. Enlarged conversation with an audience compels you to think, not primarily about yourself but about your listeners. Present your ideas to *them*. Interest *them*. Watch for *their* response. Better than talking to them is talking *with* them. When you talk *with* them you watch to see that they have understood each point before you pass to the next.

Let us be frank about this. It takes both courage and self-control to talk earnestly with an audience. "It is four-fifths will power," admitted one speaker after he really had learned how. You have to face it somewhere along the way. If you weaken, and back up inside, you lose control of yourself—and lose control of your audience. Hence those speakers who mumble, or stare at the floor, or gaze out the window. They lack courage and self-control; or having only a little of either, they talk in that infamous *half*-direct way. "Style," said Arthur Schopenhauer, "is the physiognomy of the mind, and a safer index to character than the face." This is even more true of delivery than of style. In a round-about way, then, we are saying that listeners have the right to demand that speakers be persons of character, persons who have earned the right to speak, persons who will make it worth while for others to listen.

[1] James A. Winans, *Public Speaking* (New York: Appleton-Century-Crofts, Inc., 1915), p. 31.

SIR ANTHONY EDEN, PIERRE MENDÈS-FRANCE, AND
JOHN FOSTER DULLES

They have met in Paris to talk an international problem into solution.

A HIPPOCRATIC OATH FOR PUBLIC SPEAKERS

Since democracy, as Macaulay put it, is "Government by speaking," a standard of responsibility ought to be demanded of its speakers. A totalitarian state can coerce, but a democracy must persuade. In it issues are aired, "talked out of existence or talked into solution." The persons who do the talking, then, ought to be held accountable for their manner of talk. We have progressed to a stage where no citizens are permitted to practice law or medicine without passing an examination to test their fitness. Examinations usually are also required of such persons as engineers, public accountants, and taxicab drivers. We might imagine a truly Ideal Republic in which a test of competence was also required before persons were allowed to practice the art of public speaking. They would be required, first, to show that they were capable of producing ideas, and, further, that they were capable of refining them into a form fit for human consumption. Finally, they would be required to demonstrate a mastery of that complicated process so glibly called "delivery," of translating thought from speaker to audience.

Having passed these tests of professional competence, then in the Ideal Republic would come the oath of moral responsibility, a Hippocratic oath in which each citizen certified to speak in public would make the following vow: *"I swear in the name of God and my own conscience that I will never speak in public unless I have prepared myself with substance worth saying, and unless further I have put it into form that can be understood. I further swear that when I appear before an audience I shall think of its welfare and not of my own pride, that I shall not mumble or fidget, or otherwise evade or shirk my task, but shall present my ideas with such sincerity, earnestness, and consideration for the audience that none can fail to hear or comprehend."*

Such would be indeed an Ideal Republic. In the chapters that follow we shall consider how a speaker could learn to fulfill this vow.

Chapter 2

DEVELOPING THE MENTAL
ATTITUDE FOR GOOD SPEAKING

In the first chapter we referred to speakers who fidget, mumble, or talk as though reciting from a copy-book. Behind these and other common causes of failure is the speaker's poor mental attitude. " 'Tis hard for an empty bag to stand upright," observed Benjamin Franklin. The trouble is not with the bag, but from the lack of real stuff inside it. So with speakers.

The Sense of Communication

"I knew a very distinguished man once," said Clarence B. Randall, "who memorized every word of each address, and did it with amazing skill, but I always felt that his slight preoccupation with the effort of memory drew an unfortunate veil between him and his audience." Randall's judgment deserves respect. He is not only a former Godkin lecturer and recipient of a U. S. Speaker-of-the-Year Award; he is also one of the most discerning analysts on where and why speaking in American public life is effective, and where and why it is impotent. There is nothing inherently wrong with memorizing, of course. Actors memorize, and many earlier speakers memorized. They spent years in learning the art, and weeks in rehearsing and perfecting memory for each performance. People in earlier centuries admired the art of memorizing, and applauded one who perfected the art. They applauded often for the art itself. Not so today. The tempo of this twentieth century industrial civilization simply does not fit that kind of speaking. Audiences do not admire speeches primarily as an art. They want information on the swift changes taking place in the world around them. They want to hear the strongly-held convictions of the speaker as he stands before them. He won't reach them by reciting polished memorized phrases. He won't lead them, or influence their thinking, until he projects himself directly into their minds. You can sum it up in one word. In real public speaking you *communicate*. Memorizers almost never communicate. They recite, and the "unfortunate veil" hangs between them and the audience.

The same is true with using notes and manuscripts. The brain that is searching for the next reminder is momentarily cut off from the listener, and in that moment mind-to-mind contact is broken. Each time it is broken it has to be re-established. "There is no gesture in the world," said Clarence B. Randall, "more persuasive with an audience than for the speaker after he has addressed the chair to turn out the reading light. No one can doubt that such a man is voicing his own opinions, and no matter how bad his phrasing or how broken his sentences, there is a rugged integrity about what he says that can be deeply moving. When he looks them in the eye and lets them have it they listen, and they respect him even when they differ." [1]

Let us grant freely that most speakers today use notes or manuscript. Let us grant that some do it well, and a few superbly. The bald fact remains that most do it badly.

We talk a great deal of the differences between public speaking and private conversation. Actually, the differences are largely superficial and the likenesses are fundamental. How do they differ? Where is the dividing line between them? How sharp is it? James A. Winans in his *Public Speaking* raises the issue in a vivid way. He imagines a man who has been in a great battle, or is fired with a great enthusiasm, meeting a friend on the street and pausing to talk. Others gather; he lifts his voice that all may hear. Still others gather; and they wish to see as well as hear him, so he mounts a cart and goes on with his talk. Obviously, the man started with a conversation and ended with a public speech. Where, asks Winans, did the conversation become a public speech?

We might pick any given place as the passover point. We could say that conversation becomes public speaking when the number of listeners reaches 10, or when it reaches 50, or when the speaker stands on a cart or platform. But these obviously are arbitrary points. None represents a fundamental distinction.

Actually, conversation *gradually* becomes public speaking, and public speaking is simply *enlarged* conversation. So get rid of the

[1] Clarence B. Randall, *Freedom's Faith* (Boston, Little, Brown and Company, 1953), p. 142. The quotation in the preceding paragraph is from p. 145.

idea that when you stand on a platform you are "making a speech." You are not declaiming. You are not unloading an idea. You are not talking to the walls, or ceiling, or simply into the air. You are not even talking *at* the audience. You are talking *to* the people, and there should be no dreamy look in your face or far-away tone in your voice. You are talking *with* the people, and you should learn early to observe their responses while you talk. Plainly they will say to you, "I agree, go ahead," or "I don't quite understand that; make it clearer," or "I am bored; will you please stop."

Enlarged conversation, of course, presents definite problems. Not all people are good conversationalists. Some bore you in private speech, and on the platform their speaking amounts to mass boredom. These present a delicate problem in class, for when the instructor comments on their tiresome tones they are likely to reply honestly and innocently, "But that's the way I naturally talk." Shall the instructor tactfully avoid the issue? Or shall he say with brutal honesty: "Exactly. That's the trouble. In private conversation you bore two or three. In public speech you bore thirty." Other people speak passably well in private, but public enlargement brings out cracks and flaws. All in all, then, we should look at some of the attributes of good enlarged conversation:

LOOKING THE AUDIENCE IN THE MIND

Did you ever observe people in earnest conversation, really observe them closely? They don't gaze out the window, or at the floor, or at the ceiling. They look one another directly in the eye. This eye directness, however, is only an outward sign of inward state of mind. Mentally they are trying to look each other in the mind.

This is the mental attitude of the good public speaker, no matter how large the audience or how small. His manner may vary to fit the occasion. His posture, action, and voice may change to fit the size of the audience or the formality of the occasion. The one thing he does not change is his direct looking-the-audience-in-the-mind mode of communication. Adam Smith, that great university lecturer of the eighteenth century, will serve as an example. He was great because he spoke not only to the patient ear of the earnest student, but also to the shallow ear of the poorest student, and to the callous ear of the great world outside, "which must be tickled in order to be made attentive." He attributed his success, said his biographer, "very largely to the vigilant care with which he watched his audience; for he depended very much upon their sympathy. 'During one whole session,' he is reported to have said, 'a certain student with a plain but expressive countenance was of great use to me in judging my success. . . . If he leant forward to listen, all was right; but if he leant back in an attitude of listlessness I felt at once that all was wrong, and that I must change either the subject or the style of my address.' " [2]

BEING EARNEST

Some speakers talk as though spraying water over a garden with a hose. They spray the words into the air over the audience, and the words fall like drops of water. Word-spraying is not communicative because the word-sprayer is not speaking earnestly.

Above all else, a good speaker must be in earnest. "An audience," says James A. Winans, "will forgive a speaker almost any lack, if he is manifestly earnest. . . . Earnestness moves our emotions, thaws our indifference, and gives us faith which a leader must create."

It is not easy for a speaker to be in earnest the first time he stands before an audience. He has not had enough experience with this sort of thing. He stands up alone, like a man before a firing squad, and the eyes of the audience gleam at him like shining gun barrels. He wishes he were home, or in a foxhole on a battlefield, or anywhere else than standing here alone and unprotected from those gleaming eyes. Under the circumstances, he tends to do one of two wrong things: Either he shrinks within himself to escape those terrible eyes, and talks in a small voice that cannot be sufficiently heard; or he fights back, and bellows defiantly in loud tones so as to prove he is not afraid.

Neither of these is communicative speaking, and both come from the wrong mental attitude. Uppermost in a speaker's mind—even in the first speech he ever makes—should be this concept: "I am here to tell this audience about this subject, and I want to tell them in the same way I would in a very important private conversation. I must magnify and intensify my tone and manner. I must reach them all, even on the back row. I must make them see this subject and feel about it as I do. To do this I must talk to them and with them. Above all I must be earnest."

PERSONALIZED SPEAKING AND THE RHYTHM OF TALK

In private conversation we use those personal pronouns—"we," and "you," and "I." We also use "talking words," those short words

[2] Francis W. Hirst, *Adam Smith* (London, Macmillan Company, 1904), pp. 34-35.

BISHOP FULTON J. SHEEN

His televised talks on "Life Is Worth Living," are superior examples of personalized speaking.

DuMont Television

DR. NORMAN VINCENT PEALE

His Intimate Study Chats are superior examples of looking the audience in the mind.

Wide World

of the English language known to everybody. Thus when talking we commonly say *but* instead of "however," *go* instead of "travel," *think* instead of "reflect," and *want* instead of "desire."

Communicative public speakers also use those personal pronouns and talking words. For most students this presents a critical problem. They write their speeches, or write their outlines, and these written speeches and outlines *sound* written. They avoid talking words, and use the longer, more abstract words like "however," "travel," "reflect," and "desire." They avoid personal pronouns. Instead of saying "I think," they back in, crab-like, with "It is my thought that." Worse, they tend to circle around an idea with what they mistakenly think is fitting written language, like this:

> It is my desire to reveal how the early environmental factors in Bernard Shaw developed the ability to produce the plays that he wrote.

In plain talk this means:

> I want to show how Bernard Shaw's early environment influenced the plays he wrote later.

Personalized speaking is not a problem of word choice but of mental attitude. The student who avoids talking words and personal pronouns is not a communicative speaker. He is simply reciting a written essay, and one not well written at that.

Finally, there is the rhythm of talk. We think in contractions and in private conversation we speak in contractions. We say "I *don't*," not "I do not," and we say "*it's*," not "it is." Only when we want to emphasize a negative do we say "He is *not* here." As Dorothy McCleary, prize-winning novelist and master of dialogue writing, says, "It is only persons who are unsure of the language who use the full forms of speech, because they lack the intimate feel for the contraction." (She would include also those pedants afflicted by excess precision.) Here is the nub, for stage-frightened students giving a public speech *are* unsure of their language; hence they tend to avoid contractions, and hence they sound artificial.

This use of contractions is the basis of speech rhythm. One reason (though not the only one) why most people sound artificial when they try to read is that they don't use contractions, but use the full written speech forms. The result is a stilted speech rhythm. To compare stilted rhythm with genuine speech rhythm, read aloud the following passage without using contractions:

I know it is said that the rule of the majority is the rule of the stupid. I do not believe it.

Now read it again, using the contractions that permit speech rhythm:

I know it's said that the rule of the majority is the rule of the stupid. I don't believe it.

Now read it still again, this time not only using contractions but also giving full emphasis to the important words and unstressing the less important ones:

I know it's *said* / thatth' *rule* uvth' *majority* / izth' rule uvth' *stupid* / I *don't believe* it /

Read in this way, it sounds like real talk, not like recitation.

PHYSICAL VITALITY

Enlarged conversation demands also what seems to the beginning speaker like an unbelievable amount of physical vitality, so much that at first they simply do not believe it. Talking to one or two persons close by requires relatively little energy. Listless conversation requires almost no energy. But when you speak to twenty people in a classroom, or a hundred in an auditorium, it requires *five, ten, fifty, or a hundred times the energy of good private conversation* in order for the speaker's voice to sound as loud, earnest, and direct as in good private conversation.[3]

The speaker who talks earnestly to a public audience, therefore, is a fountain of vital force. He opens his mouth wider than he ever would dream of doing in private conversation, and he makes sure that even those farthest away can hear him easily. He communicates uninhibitedly with head, body, and arms. This is the compulsion necessitated by "enlarged" conversation.

[3] The following pertinent data is taken from L. S. Judson and A. T. Weaver, *Voice Science* (New York, Appleton-Century-Crofts, Inc., 1942), pp. 285-288:

1. Speech power:

of soft whisper	0.001	microwatts
of soft speech	0.1	microwatts
of average speech	15.0	microwatts
of loud speech	1000.0	microwatts

Thus loud speech requires 66 times the power of average speech, 10,000 times the power of soft speech, and 1,000,000 times the power of soft whisper.

2. Sound intensity and distance: The intensity of sound varies inversely as the square of the distance from the source. A speaker, let us assume, produces a sound of given intensity at a certain distance. At twice the distance this sound has one-fourth the original intensity, and at three times the distance it has only one-ninth the original intensity.

The Sense of Humor

.At the risk of being misunderstood, we list a sense of humor as an important attribute of a speaker's mental attitude.

First, let us see what is meant by *sense of humor*. The term *humor* is used frequently to mean the same thing as *fun*. Sometimes it is used synonymously with *wit*. As used here, however, it is distinguished from both. Fun and wit have their proper places in public talk as well as in conversation, but neither takes the place of humor.

Webster's Dictionary of Synonyms defines *humor* as implying "more human sympathy, more tolerance, more kindliness than *wit*, . . . a feeling for the not readily perceived pathos as well as for the not readily perceived absurdness of characters, of situations, of consequences." *Wit* is defined as " intellectual brilliancy and quickness of perception combined with the talent for expressing one's ideas in a sparkling effective manner." *Fun,* of course, is "a natural or inherent capacity for laughing, for provoking laughter, or for finding a cause for laughter in other persons." Thus *fun* suggests boisterous laughter; and *wit* denotes intellectual subtlety, often sharp and biting; but *humor* is gentle and understanding and sympathetic. Hence we speak of the *fun* of playing children; and writers distinguish the *wit* of Dryden and Pope from the *humor* of Shakespeare.

Let us look beneath the surface of humor. On what is it based? Real humor springs from deep insight, an insight that includes more than knowledge, for it adds understanding and wisdom. Fanatics are lacking in humor because they lack perspective. Hence they become not merely serious, but solemn. They are zealots, often unable to laugh or even smile, and, significantly, unable to see their subject in the light of fairness.

Someone has listed the ten most common subjects of jokes. The list includes the most serious things in life. Death itself stands near the top. Marriage, divorce, and like subjects follow closely. The startling fact is that we make jokes about things that certainly are not in themselves funny. Why? We simply learn to see them in perspective. Life is important, but countless people have thrown it away for something they considered more important. Death is serious, but countless people have met it with a smile.

One whose humor is in good repair has a truer and saner view of his world. The speaker with a sense of humor, one who can be amused at his own stage fright, who can see the sunlight of laughter in human problems as well as the serious side, is one to whom an audience is instinctively drawn. It is his guarantee of mental balance. People recognize in him a sane leader and in him they put more trust.

A Sense of Leadership and Self-respect

In a true sense the speaker is a *leader*. He cannot escape the implications of leadership. What do they imply?

To gain the respect of others, a leader must respect himself. You wish to be believed? Then believe in yourself. You may say: But I don't believe in myself; I have doubts and fears about the whole business! Of course; and so does every speaker and every leader during those long years of growth; only they have learned with Emerson that "Do the thing you fear and the death of fear is certain." Within reasonable limits self-respect can be cultivated, if you cultivate the foundations on which to base it. How?

First, *prepare thoroughly*. If you have not really prepared the speech, you don't deserve self-respect, and down in your own heart you know it. If you have not earned the right to speak, you have not earned the right to self-respect. If you have waited until the night before, and then are wondering frantically what to do, it is time to take an honest inventory of yourself. Self-respect must be earned.

Second, *get enthusiastic about your subject*. Enthusiasm is not a rare quality, but it is a precious one. Without it, speaking—and life itself —would lose much of its interest and meaning. We can almost say that without it speaking is futile. Certainly it cannot rise above the level of routine; and routine speaking is seldom heard with pleasure. Said Emerson, "Nothing great was ever achieved without enthusiasm." Without enthusiasm, speaking is barely tolerable.

Third, *act as if you had complete self-respect and confidence*. Emotions and mental attitudes can be induced by deliberately assuming the physical positions and by going through the actions that characterize such emotions and attitudes. Double up your fists, grit your teeth, stomp the floor, and frown—all the while thinking of something that naturally provokes your wrath—and you can work yourself into a fair state of anger. Or smile, relax your muscles, and think of something cheerful, and you can go a long way toward getting rid of a grouch. In the same way, stand straight, chest up and

eyes to the front, and think how important it is that people believe
you, and you will tend to acquire that self-respect and confidence
without which there is no good speaking.

Fourth, *be careful not to overdo self-respect!* Carried too far, it
can become egotism or conceit. "For by the grace given to me I bid
every one among you not to think of himself more highly than he
ought to think, but to think with sober judgment." Achieve if you
can full self-respect, tempered with fitting modesty. Don't, on the
one hand, stand with a metaphorical "please kick me" sign pinned
to your coattail, or act, on the other hand, as if you had, with some
assistance from God, created the universe.

Overcoming Stage Fright

"How can I overcome stage fright?" is perhaps the most frequently
asked of all questions about public speaking. The fear of an audience
besets speakers young and old.

This problem in mental relationship between speaker and audience
has deliberately been deferred to last. The truth is that by deferring
it we have been able to cover most of the problems relating to stage
fright without having to face the matter head on, and that is the way
stage fright ought to be handled. It is a negative thing, a fear, and
you cannot fight a fear without soon fearing the fear itself. The approach to mastering stage fright is a *positive* one and we have already
covered it in this chapter. The speaker who acquires a Sense of Communication, who maintains a Sense of Humor, and who develops a
reasonable Sense of Leadership will not suffer unduly from stage
fright. He will not overcome it—he ought not to overcome it as we
shall see in a moment—but he will be able to live with it, and even
to speak better because of it.

You should know that stage fright is the usual sensation of persons
who perform in public. Lily Pons, after twenty-five years of concert
singing, "feels faintly seasick all day before a concert or opera performance." The actress, Eva Le Gallienne, after she had just rounded
out her one-thousandth repertory performance, was asked by an in-
terviewer if she experienced stage fright. She answered, "Yes. And it
gets worse every year." When Abraham Lincoln went to Washington
as a Congressman, at the age of thirty-six, he wrote home that during
his speeches in Congress, "I was about as badly scared, and no worse,
as I am when I speak in court." Even Cicero, more than two thousand

years ago, struggled with stage fright and left us a record of his feelings (he attributes the words to Crassus but is describing his own
feelings): "I turn pale at the outset of a speech, and quake in every
limb and in all my soul."

But stage fright if properly controlled *helps* the speaker instead of
hinders. What Amelita Galli-Curci said of singers is just as true of
speakers: "The person who does not get the least bit nervous at the
prospect of stepping on the stage will never move an audience to wild
ecstasy." Cicero had discovered this twenty centuries ago: "For the
better the speaker, the more profoundly is he frightened of the difficulty of speaking, and of the doubtful fate of a speech, and of the
anticipations of an audience." Cicero did not know *why* this was true,
but modern psychologists have discovered why. Stage fright, they
have found, is accompanied by chemical changes in the blood, the
most important being the excessive secretion of adrenalin (and possibly of thyroxin). But psychologists have further discovered that
adrenalin is also secreted by vigorous bodily action, even in the absence of stage fright or other emotion. Finally, they have discovered
that these physiological changes, if they are controlled and directed,
"increase our adequacy" of performance. In other words, a reasonable amount of stage fright, if controlled and directed, makes you a
better speaker.

Your problem, then, is not how to overcome stage fright, but how
to reduce it, control it, and give better speeches because of it. There
is no formula for this, but there are four tested procedures.

GET AN INTERESTING SUBJECT

Ask yourself, first of all, whether you are afraid of your audience
or are really afraid of your subject. Many students are afraid of
their subject, and for a good reason. They don't *know* much about it.
They don't *care* much about it. But a speech is coming up, and they've
got to have a subject, so they picked this one—a bit desperately
perhaps—and are going through the motions with it. They don't have
stage fright. They have subject fright.

Stay off dry and dusty subjects, and avoid talking about something
simply because "it might be a good subject." Instead, get a subject
that really interests you, one that fires you up when you think of it.
Ask yourself: What do I mostly think about when I am not working?
(There you have a *good* subject.) Or ask: Which course in college do
I like most of all, and why? Which do I like least, and why? Or ask:

What outside activity do I like most? (Here are three more good subjects.)

BE WELL PREPARED

Said Charles W. Lomas after some ten years of investigating causes and case histories of stage fright: *"Many of these cases of severe stage fright are simply the result of inadequate preparation, sometimes without the student himself being aware of it.* He may, for example, have simply memorized something that he has not made his own. The slightest distraction may destroy his set of cues, and he has not sufficient knowledge of the material to reconstruct them. Or he may have crammed his preparation into the period immediately preceding the speech class, or he may have tired himself by late hours in preparation the night before. To the student it will look as though sufficient time had been spent to insure mastery of the speech situation. But the same amount of time spread over several days would give him a far better grasp of the material and more assurance before the audience." [4]

USE PHYSICAL ACTION

The person who has stage fright is physically tense all over. This tension is not merely the effect of fear; it is also in part the cause of fear. One is not simply tense because he is afraid; but in part *he is afraid because he is tense.* He is caught in a vicious circle: Because he is afraid he becomes tense, and because he becomes tense he becomes still more afraid. At some point he must break this vicious circle.

To prescribe a cure is easy. Simply *relax.* Use only those muscles needed to keep the body poised and erect, and relax all others. Free the tension in the arms, in the hands, and, above all, in the face. In short, get the tonus of the body back to normal, and stage fright will be reduced.

This, of course, cannot be done by merely commanding the body to relax. It can be done by *doing* something with the head, hands, and feet. Take a step or two, no matter how heroic an effort it requires. Nod the head, or shake it. Smile, or at least raise the eyebrows. Use the hands in some way or other. Then the instant any part of the body is free, use it to help carry your thought to the audience. Remember that mere vigorous action is not enough; it may fly off at

[4] Charles W. Lomas, "Stage Fright," *Quarterly Journal of Speech*, XXX (December, 1944), p. 483.

loose ends, and you may merely pace the floor, fumble at your clothes, and scratch your face. To relieve stage fright and drain it away, you need to break the tension and *use vigorous action for communicating your thought to the audience.* Once this is done, you will be freed from the grip of fear, and ultimately there will come to you that great sense of self-mastery, the triumph of knowing you have not only overcome, but have put to use, the very force that held you fast.

DON'T THINK OF YOURSELF, BUT OF YOUR SUBJECT AND AUDIENCE

Perhaps the majority of frustrated people in the world are victims of the inability to forget themselves. Among these is the speaker who keeps asking himself, "How am I doing?" for putting your mind on "How am I doing?" tends to make you self-conscious and muscle-bound, and helps to manufacture stage fright.

> A centipede was happy quite
> Until a frog in fun
> Said, "Pray, which leg comes after which?"
> This raised her mind to such a pitch,
> She lay distracted in a ditch,
> Considering how to run.

During much of our lives we think of ourselves, but if we would speak effectively we need what Ralph Dennis called "a vivid sense of the brotherhood of man." We need to lose ourselves in the welfare of those to whom we talk. Can they hear us? Can they understand us? Are we throwing light on problems that puzzle them? He speaks well who gives something of *himself* to the audience. He speaks not well who thinks too much *about* himself—and stage fright will not be his only problem.

Exercises

1. Hear a speech and write a brief report on the speaker's directness, earnestness, rhythm of talk, and vitality. Before hearing this speaker, better make a brief outline of the suggestions contained in that part of this chapter. Then you can check the speaker against these items.

2. Write a report on your stage fright during the previous speech, covering the following points:

   a. How it affected you (rapid heart beat, dry mouth, trembling, weak voice, etc.).

   b. How you used the four tested procedures for reducing stage fright:

      1) Why you chose your subject, and whether it was a good one.

      2) How long ahead you started preparing it, and how you prepared it.

      3) How many times you rehearsed it, and whether you rehearsed posture and physical action.

      4) Whom you thought most about during the speech: "How am I doing?" or "Are my listeners getting this?"

3. In reading aloud the following selection, forget yourself, your nervousness, your stage fright, and *think wholly of communicating the thought and mood to your listeners:*

There has been a trend recently toward what is called "leadership"—but what is really nothing more than the idolation of individual men. In Italy, Mussolini took the title of Il Duce—the Leader—on the grounds that he was the one man who could fulfill the destiny of the Italian people. Not long after, in Germany, Hitler began calling himself Der Führer. . . .

I do not know all the reasons for this emphasis on single individuals. But I do perceive a connection, here in America at any rate, between that emphasis and the neglect of the liberal arts. Had we more faith in liberal education, we would have, I believe, more faith in ourselves—more faith in the great leavening process of democracy, which forever pushes new men to the top.

I have had the privilege of meeting most of the great men of our time and of conversing with them intimately. . . . Yet I can say truthfully that, however impressive their abilities—and I have found them impressive—I saw nothing in them that could not conceivably be duplicated in Akron, Ohio, where I practiced law for many years, or here at Duke University. I think it was William Howard Taft who said you could find a man fit to sit on the Supreme Court Bench of the United States, in any town in America of more than 5,000 population. Possibly Mr. Taft exaggerated. Yet surely the *principle* has been proved time after time in American history. The vast American educational system has set men free—free not alone to serve, but free to lead. Education is the mother of leadership.

Wendell L. Willkie, "Freedom and the Liberal Arts."

Chapter 3

FIRST STEPS IN MANAGING IDEAS

T he first step in managing ideas is to get ideas to manage. But getting ideas is not easy, for you don't prepare a speech in the same way you work twenty problems in algebra or study thirty pages of history.

Speeches grow. They grow and ripen. "No great thing," said Epictetus, "is created suddenly, any more than a bunch of grapes or a fig. If you tell me that you want a fig, I answer you that there must be time. Let it first blossom, then bear fruit, then ripen."

Some people find it incredible that a speech must blossom, bear fruit, then ripen. "Good speakers," they argue, "can talk off the cuff." Such a notion is pure fantasy, however much shallow minds want to believe it. Said Louis XIV to Jean Baptiste Massillon: "Father, I have heard a great many orators in this chapel, and have been highly pleased with them; but for you, whenever I hear you, I go away displeased with myself, for I see more of my own character." The sermons that so influenced Louis were written and rewritten many times. Franklin D. Roosevelt, a speaker of consummate skill, drew freely on others, then drafted each speech through five to twelve revisions. Winston Churchill, probably the most effective British speaker of the past two centuries, prepared speeches thoroughly and painstakingly, sometimes using two secretaries in relays to type his dictation. After his elaborate notes were in final shape, recorded his biographer, Robert Louis Taylor, he "then rehearses them before a mirror in order to study his gestures. Moreover, he records them on a machine, then edits for clarity, voice inflexion, tone quality and general structure." At the close of his study of eminent speakers, Sir Austen Chamberlain wrote: "Those who say to public men, 'Oh, speaking is no trouble to *you*,' have not seen them in the hours of preparation. Their wives and their private secretaries tell a different tale."

A good part of every college speech course is wasted by some students who try to speak without earning the right. Their speeches are poor—not because they are beginners and not because they cannot learn or have no talent—but because they do not put forth the effort. Months go by, and a large part of the course is gone, and they have yet not learned one simple fundamental—that a speaker must earn the right to give a speech.

These first steps in managing ideas, then, are really first steps in earning the right to speak. You cannot wait to study all the speech principles before making your first speech, so we shall here start with simple speeches and elementary procedures:

    1. Choose a subject of interest to you, and one that can be made interesting to the audience.

    2. Do not try to cover the whole subject, but select one specific part for your central idea.

    3. Phrase the central idea into a Purpose-Sentence so you will know where you are going.

    4. Make a list of two or three main points of your central idea, or not more than four at the most.

    5. Obtain specific and interesting material to support each of these main points.

    6. Organize the speech into an outline.

    7. Practice delivering the speech until you have it well in mind.

Choose a Subject of Interest to You, and One That Can Be Made Interesting to the Audience

Where can I find an interesting subject? you ask. Not so fast, if you please. Look first at your audience. They are college students, mostly about your own age. They are not business executives or labor leaders, and you cannot talk to them as such. They are not high-school students, so you cannot work off on them that speech you prepared back in high school. These college students have a wide range of interests. Some might be called scholars; they are interested in books and ideas. Some are athletes; and it is a subject very much on their minds. Some are interested in science; and much of their time is spent in a laboratory. Some are interested in the humanities; for them literature and languages are life's deepest current. Some are going to become engineers, teachers, lawyers, physicians, house-wives.

You may ask how anyone can find a subject to fit people with such a wide variety of interests. Really a wide range of subjects can be made interesting to such people. If stimulated they have eternally questing minds. Already in college they are specializing, and most of them have an uneasy feeling that outside their field of study are many things they ought to know about. Terence, the Roman playwright, brought thunderous applause with his line, "I am a man and interested in all *manly* things." So are the college students in your audience.

Here are guides for finding subjects to interest them:

1. Choose a subject you know something about already, and about which you can find out more.

2. Choose a subject the audience may know a little about, but wants to know more.

Are you majoring in literature? Tell the class who the newest writers are, and what they are trying to do. Or what is blank verse, and why writers use it. Or who was Homer? Or why Poe lived in travail?

Are you majoring in economics or business? A wealth of subjects is yours: taxes, prices, profits, wages, social security, government finance, labor laws. . .

Are you a science major? Then explain to the class what sonic speed is, and why it was once a hazard to airplanes. Or how radar works. Or what is the difference between a virus and a germ. Or why scientists study the lower forms of animal life. Or what Pasteur did.

Are you an athlete? Then increase your hearers' understanding of games and pleasure in watching them. Explain types of offense and defense, what spectators should look for, and how they can get greater enjoyment from knowing the finer points of games.

Do Not Try to Cover the Whole Subject, But Select One Specific Part for Your Central Idea

Young speakers are likely at first to cover the moon, the sand, and the stars in a five-minute speech. The coverage is thin. Narrow the subject until you can cover it specifically.

Is your subject art? Behold a speech that tries to cover all:

> Greek and Roman art
> Italian masters
> Dutch, Flemish, and French painters
> English and American painters
> Oriental art
> The Moderns: Realism, Surrealism, etc.
> Why we have art

For a classroom speech you might settle for a fraction of the last topic:

> How lines and colors can improve your looks

Is your subject Communism? Here is a speech that tries to cover too much:

> Karl Marx
> Communism in Russia
> Communism in other parts of Europe and Asia
> Communism in the United States

From this vast area you might choose the following central idea that would interest everybody:

> Latest changes of policy in the State Department for combating world Communist aggression

A good speech is not unlike a good photograph. It is in focus; and a good close-up is better than a hazy distant-shot.

Phrase the Central Idea Into a Purpose-Sentence So You Know Where You Are Going

As this is stated you may not at first see what it means, or why you should do it. Yet it is important, and if you don't do it you can later run into trouble. It is important because a speech, unlike a private conversation, needs a definite purpose. A private conversation may be aimless, but a good public speech moves definitely toward a goal. The speaker is going somewhere. He knows in advance where he is going. He wants the audience to *know* something, to *understand* something, to *believe* something, to *do* something. Therefore, to keep in mind where your speech is going, put it down in writing.

You are going to talk on football, let us assume, and have selected the following central idea:

The type of offense used by our team this year

With such a central idea you may have any one of several purposes, as indicated by the following Purpose-Sentences:

I want to increase your enjoyment in watching football by explaining the type of offense being used this year by our team [i. e., *information*], or

The type of football offense used by the team this year is superior to that used last year [i.e., *argument*], or

The type of football offense used by the team this year is superior to that used by our major opponents [i.e., *argument*].

Now any one of these three could be a good speech purpose, but do not try to wander across all three of them in a single speech. Choose *one*, write it out in a clear cut Purpose-Sentence, and hold to it as you plan the speech.

AVOID ARGUMENT AND CONTROVERSY IN YOUR FIRST SPEECHES

A final suggestion: For your first speeches, better avoid subjects involving argument and controversy. At its best, argument is an explosive and you have to know how to handle it. *"Win an argument and you lose a soul,"* said Bishop Fulton J. Sheen. There will be plenty of time later for speeches on controversial subjects, but start first with the fundamentals—and the most fundamental thing in speaking is to be able to *explain something clearly to your listeners in a way that will interest them.*

Make a List of Two or Three Main Points of Your Central Idea, or Not More Than Four at the Most

These main points should cover the whole central idea. Later (pages 83-87) we shall take up the thought patterns for arranging main topics, but for the present rely on common sense plus what you already know about composition. Make your main points simple and obvious. Also, do not have too many of them, for listeners cannot remember too many. Generally speaking, five are too many. Other things being equal, three are better than four, and two are better than three.

For example, your first draft might have five main points like this:

PURPOSE-SENTENCE: You can improve your looks by the proper use of lines
                    and colors.

Main Points: I. People should know how to look their best.
                       II. Stout people can be helped by artistic lines.
                      III. Thin people can also be helped.
                       IV. One set of colors enhances dark eyes and hair.
                        V. Another set of colors enhances blue eyes and light
                           hair.

Here are too many main points, and they are spread too thin. (This
is often true when a speech has too many main points.) A better
arrangement would reduce them to two main points, as follows:

PURPOSE-SENTENCE: You can improve your looks by the proper use of lines
                    and colors.

Main Points: I. If you are either fat or thin, skillful use of *lines* can
                           improve your looks.
                       II. If you are either blond or brunette, you can be
                           helped by knowing which *colors* to wear.

Note the improvement: First, there are two main points instead of
five. Second, both points are easy for listeners to remember (and
remember they hear the speaker's words only once), for one deals
with *lines* and the other with *colors.*

Obtain Specific and Interesting Material to Support Each of These Main Points

In the main points you state an idea or a principle. Technically
these are known as *Assertions.* An Assertion does not elaborate,
explain, or prove. It only asserts. But in speechmaking Assertion is
not enough, for no idea or principle can hang in the air unsupported.
To assert that "older people have an unfair advantage over youth
because they have lived longer," or that "Ernest Hemingway is a
great writer," hangs unsupported in the air. It does not in itself
increase our knowledge or change our belief. Standing alone, it is "as
broad and general as the casing air." Its content is too large for us
to comprehend it in a statement. Or if we did understand, sheer inertia would prevent our thinking from being altered by an isolated
assertion. Most important, we seldom remember unsupported Assertions. We hear the speaker's words but once. Unlike a reader, we
cannot pause to think back or to reread. We must go right on, keeping
pace with the speaker's words at a continuous and unbroken rate. Of

the speeches you hear, how much do you remember? Certainly not many of the unsupported Assertions. They are like drifting clouds. They may catch our attention for the moment, but we do not remember them easily one from another.

What do we remember? We remember things that are kept vividly before our minds. We remember ideas that are supported by a succession of details, by examples, by comparisons, by illustrations. We remember ideas that are *hammered in.*

HOW TO USE SUPPORTING MATERIAL

One of the speaker's main tasks, therefore, is to support his Assertions with effective material. For the present we shall consider the following five kinds of supporting materials:

1. Facts and Figures
2. Specific Instances
3. Illustrations
4. Comparisons
5. Testimony

The manner of using these supporting materials can be seen in the following cross section of an outline:

1. ASSERTION

    A. Supporting material
    B. Supporting material

The speech might be more elaborate, of course, and have two or more levels of Assertions. But a good speech, no matter how many levels of Assertions it has, gets down in the end to the bedrock of supporting materials. The following is a cross section of outline for *two* levels of Assertion:

1. ASSERTION (FIRST LEVEL)

    A. *Assertion (second level)*

        1. Supporting material
        2. Supporting material

    B. *Assertion (second level)*

        1. Supporting material
        2. Supporting material

KINDS OF SUPPORTING MATERIAL

FACTS AND FIGURES

This is the most elementary type of supporting material, plain Facts and Figures. Yet student speeches are notably weak in Facts and Figures. In general, students don't get the pertinent facts and don't use what few facts they have. They rely on Assertion, as if anyone cared about their Assertions unsupported. Therefore make this your basic rule: Where Facts and Figures are to be had, get them, verify them, and use them. Beware of alleged facts. Remember that much printed material today is deliberately planted for propaganda. The "facts" may be accurate (though not always), but their selection —and careful omissions—make them misleading. Check your sources! A first test of educated people is to read suspiciously, and know how to detect propaganda.

The following example demonstrates the use of verified facts as supporting material:

MAIN POINT (ASSERTION): I. The three best-selling American novels have no common element that explains their popularity.

Facts and Figures   A. *Uncle Tom's Cabin* was a tale of slavery, written in the pre-Civil War turmoil; it sold 3,000,000 copies.

Facts and Figures   B. *Ben Hur* was a tale of the Christ, written in the Gilded Age of boom-and-bust-and-dollar-chasing in the late 19th century; it sold 2,500,000 copies.

Facts and Figures   C. *Gone With the Wind* was a story of courage in the face of disaster, written in the discouraged times of the 1930's; it sold over 4,000,000 copies.

SPECIFIC INSTANCES

By Specific Instances is meant condensed examples. These examples are brief, but specific. For them to be effective, the audience must know enough about them so they carry an instant meaning. Suppose, for example, a speaker said, "Early labor and management relations were marked by bitter strife [Assertion]. There was the Haymarket Riot, the Homestead Strike, and the Pullman Strike [Specific Instances]." These Specific Instances would not carry an instant meaning to listeners, excepting the very few who had studied labor history. Don't use that kind of Specific Instances. Use only those that listeners will understand.

The following example shows how Assertion might be supported by effective Specific Instances:

MAIN POINT (ASSERTION): I. Great achievements have been made by men and women under 30 years of age.

Specific Instance   A. At that age Elizabeth Barrett Browning had published two volumes of poems.

Specific Instance   B. Margaret Mitchell had finished half of *Gone With the Wind*.

Specific Instance   C. Lord Byron had written *Childe Harold* and published 14 volumes of poems.

Specific Instance   D. Mozart had published over 200 of his musical compositions.

Specific Instance   E. William Pitt, the Younger, had been Prime Minister of England for 6 years.

Specific Instance   F. Alexander Graham Bell had invented the telephone.

Specific Instance   G. Henry Ford had produced his first automobile.

ILLUSTRATIONS

An Illustration is a narrative of events, usually told in the order of happening. It tells the full story, but skillfully eliminates the nonessentials. As with Poe's properly constructed short story, a good Illustration will have the events so closely interwoven that not one can be removed without breaking the entire chain. A single Illustration at times is enough to support an Assertion, as in the Parable of the Good Samaritan ("And who is my neighbor?") and that of the Prodigal Son (There is joy over "one sinner that repenteth"). At other times two or more are used, as in the following example.

MAIN POINT (ASSERTION): I. The racketeers went forth, a gat in one hand and the palm of the other extended saying, "Cut me in on your business or get killed."

Illustration   A. Maxie Eisen walked into a fish market on Taylor Street, Chicago, owned by Abie the Fishman. When Abie awakened several hours later, 18 stitches had closed the revolver butt wounds in his head—

and he found himself a member of
Maxie's Retail Fish Dealers Association.
The fee for admission was $500.00.

Illustration   B. But the acme of rackets was the Master Cleaners and Dyers Union. It hired
George Bugs Moran at $1,800 a week to
make depredations on stubborn independent cleaners. When Big Tim Murphy,
who was a powerful gangster himself,
attempted to muscle in, he got one of
those $31,000 funerals. The union grew
so rich that it maintained a $700,000
defense treasury, and law-abiding people
appealed in vain to the police for protection.

COMPARISONS

Comparisons show likeness and difference between things and
ideas. Especially are they valuable supporting materials for the
following purposes:

To connect something known with something unknown. If you were
explaining, for example, how in atomic research uranium 235 was
first separated from uranium 238, you might explain how one attempt was to set up a sort of cream separator and to whirl the atoms
about until the heavier 238 units would be thrown to the outside; and
when that failed, a successful attempt was made by setting up a sort
of race track. (People know about cream separators and race tracks.)

To connect something meaningless with something meaningful. If
you say "Last year 40,000 people were killed in automobile accidents," the statement may have less meaning than if you said, "Last
year over twice as many Americans were killed in automobile
accidents as were killed in action in the Marine Corps during all its
battles of World War II." (But check such Comparisons to be sure
they are accurate. The killed-in-action figures here were checked
against the records of the Department of Defense.)

*To explain something new, about which people are suspicious,
in terms of something old which they accept.* People are often suspicious of new things, even as they were once suspicious of the printing press, of democracy, of Christianity. Therefore, when you explain
or advocate something really new, you can often best do it by showing
that it is like-this or like-that, which people already know about and
believe in. Eric Johnston used a comparison in his frank speech to

HENRY FORD II

A spokesman for management

WALTER REUTHER

A spokesman for labor

labor leaders: "Gentlemen of labor. . . You are just where we of management were ten years ago. [Then] we had everything all our own way. A friendly administration in Washington. Low taxes. And a friendly public. . . [Ten years later] you were tops. A friendly administration in Washington. All sorts of favors fed to you. . ."

The following is an outline of Comparison being used as supporting material:

MAIN POINT (ASSERTION): I. New York City is still a melting pot.

Comparison	A. It has more Irish (500,000) than Dublin.
Comparison	B. It has more Jews (2,250,000) than Israel.
Comparison	C. It has almost as many Italians (1,095,000) as Rome.
Comparison	D. It has almost as many Poles (412,000) as Warsaw.
Comparison	E. It has more Negroes (750,000) than Arkansas or Florida.

TESTIMONY

Testimony is the authority of others. In effect, the speaker says: "I am not the only one who believes this. There are two of us, or three of us, and the others are famous, or are experts, or are in a special position to know." The use of Testimony has been abused by modern advertising; for be assured that intelligent people are not impressed by the bought testimony of Strikeout Collins, baseball pitcher, on the kind of cigarettes he smokes. But intelligent people do live by authority, the right kind of authority. We accept the authority of our church, our social groups. We respect the authority of courts and judges. On questions of judgment and on complex ideas, we accept the authority of qualified experts. On reading a book we must accept, or reject, the authority of the author.

To present the Testimony of competent authorities, therefore, is one of the important methods of supporting Assertions. The following example illustrates its use:

MAIN POINT (ASSERTION): I.	Too much education consists of studying the past while ignoring the present.
Testimony	A. Thomas Jefferson warned against this danger a century and a quarter ago. At the age of 73, when many minds look backward instead of forward, Jefferson

wrote urgently that "institutions must go hand in hand with the progress of the human mind," and "as new discoveries are made. . . institutions must advance, also, and keep pace with the times"; and he warned society against remaining "ever under the regimen of their ancestors."

Testimony　　　　B. Ralph Waldo Emerson repeated the same warning a little over a hundred years ago, saying that "Each age, it is found, must write its own books."

Testimony　　　　C. Charles Francis Adams II, when he was a member of the Harvard Board of Overseers, protested to the university against the education he had received in college, because it had ignored the present and buried itself in the past: "No matter how long I may live, I shall never be able. . . to overcome some of the great disadvantages which the. . . wrong theories and worse practices of my *alma mater* inflicted upon me. And not on me alone."

USING COMBINED METHODS OF SUPPORT

Not often does a speaker limit himself to one kind of supporting material. He uses two or three of four, giving each Assertion its best variety and form of support. The following illustrates the use of *four kinds* of supporting materials for a single Assertion:

MAIN POINT (ASSERTION): I. Europe has been afflicted by barriers against money and trade.

Facts and Figures　　　　A. I don't mean the mere inconvenience of different kinds of money, for travelers get used to handling 26 cent guilders, 24 cent marks, 23 cent Swiss francs, 2 cent Belgian francs, and ¼ cent French francs.

Illustration　　　　B. One day I spent 250 Italian lira for breakfast, 9.10 Austrian shillings for lunch, and 5.05 Swiss francs for dinner; and it took only a minute to figure that in U. S. money breakfast cost 40 cents, lunch 36 cents, and dinner $1.15; that's a nuisance, but not a barrier.

Specific Instances   C. The money barrier has come from countries who fix the rate of exchange and limit the amount of their money you could take in and out: 10 pounds into England and 5 out, 200 marks into Germany and 100 out, 100 guilders into Holland and 50 out.

Specific Instances   D. The trade barriers have come, first, from high tariffs, and, second, from trade restrictions by cartels.

Testimony   E. So it was that when the Shuman Plan of 1952 removed these trade barriers by creating a West European Coal-Steel Community, its High Authority, Jean Monnet, said: "What we are doing is the greatest revolution of our history, and [it] is but the beginning."

Organize the Speech Into An Outline

A distinguished novelist, Martin Flavin, after serving as a judge in a writing contest said that as he read the new novels two things stood out. First, there was lack of plan. Second, there were too many scenes that did not advance the story but merely interrupted it. These are characteristics also of beginners' speeches, and both are inherent in the first weakness, the lack of an outline.

Anyone can learn to make an outline. Following are the basic steps:

1. Set down the Purpose-Sentence so you can keep in mind where you are going. (We have already discussed this; see pages 28-29.)

2. Make a list of the two or three main points of the central idea. (We have already discussed this; see pages 29-30.)

3. Arrange these main points in the most effective order for your audience. In doing this rely for the time being on common sense.

4. Develop each main point with specific and interesting supporting material. (For doing this, see above, pages 30-38.)

5. Plan an introduction that will explain the subject if necessary and that will capture the attention of listeners. Most introductions total about 10 per cent of the whole speech, but this proportion obviously varies.

6. Plan a conclusion that in some way will round out the speech. This may be a summary to enable listeners to remember the main points, or it

may be an illustration, quotation, or other material that leaves the listeners with a lasting impression. The average conclusion is perhaps 5 per cent of the whole speech, but obviously this also varies.

To see what a good outline looks like, turn to pages 90-97. For your first speeches you probably will find it advisable to make a rather complete outline, containing 30 to 60 per cent the number of words of the full speech. This is not a rule, of course, and each speaker will develop his own particular system. Yet by and large *responsible* speakers—as contrasted with loose talkers and demagogues—put longer and more detailed preparation on paper. Better take care at the start not to develop glibness at the expense of thoroughness and accuracy.

Practice Delivering the Speech Until You Have It Well In Mind

Each of the previous six steps has been concerned with developing ideas in your mind and getting them down on paper. You don't yet have a speech. You don't even have an "essay on its hind legs." You have only some thoughts flat on paper. Now comes the task of creating the speech out of these thoughts-on-paper. How can you create a speech while standing in front of an audience? How can you be sure, when you stand to speak, of not forgetting, of not rambling and getting ideas misplaced? How can you avoid those blank pauses, filled with *Ah* and *Er?* How can you keep within the allotted time? These are no idle questions. When you try to speak in public but the words won't come, the failure becomes real and personal.

Many people deserve to fail. This is a hard unsympathetic way of putting it, but it is true. Turning an outline into a speech requires a definite technique, which many ignore, or try to avoid by short-cuts.

First, remember that extemporaneous speaking is not impromptu speaking. To be sure, many people still think so, even as they once thought the world was flat. They think that extemporaneous speaking is speaking without preparation. This, of course, is wrong. It is completely wrong. Unprepared speeches are *impromptu,* and we are not here interested in them simply because real impromptu speeches usually are not good. Other people think that extemporaneous speeches are those "given with hasty or meager preparation." This, of course, is also wrong. It is completely wrong. These are merely poorly prepared speeches, nothing more. Wrote Winston Churchill of his first speech in Parliament, an extemporaneous speech: "It was with awe as well as eagerness that I braced myself for the supreme effort. I need not recount the pains I had taken to prepare, nor the efforts I had made to hide the work of preparation."

An extemporaneous speech is one that has been carefully thought out, carefully planned, and carefully outlined—but not written out and memorized. A speech haphazardly planned and outlined is not an extemporaneous speech. It is simply a half-breed impromptu speech—and that is the trouble with many of the so-called "extemporaneous speeches."

Next, assuming that you have a good outline, how do you convert it into a good extemporaneous speech? You have taken part in a play, or at least seen a play, so let's start from there. The actors start with a script, complete with every word set down. But the script is not the play, for the play is a *living* thing. In the same way, an outline is not the speech.

How do actors turn a script into a play? (1) They study the lines to find their meaning and their mood. (2) They learn the lines. (3) They perfect their memory and develop the play by rehearsals.

You don't follow these same steps in turning an outline into a speech, but you do use the same *process.* You don't need to study the outline to find the meaning, since you made the outline and obviously ought to know the mood and meaning of every part. Nor do you "learn the lines," as in a play, which is to say you don't memorize the speech word-for-word. Individual methods vary, but in general they use the following procedure.

MEMORIZE THE SEQUENCE OF IDEAS

First, you fix in mind the two or three main points, then fix in mind the proper sequence of supporting material. You don't memorize it formally like a poem. You don't need to have it word-perfect. You need fix in mind only the thought pattern, not the words. These are the steps which psychologists have found to be most effective:

1. First, read the outline *silently* from beginning to end. Read it slowly, feeling your way along, but don't back-track even once, for back-tracking breaks the memorizing of sequence.

2. Next, read the outline *aloud*, again without back-tracking.

3. Now put aside the outline and rehearse the speech aloud, still without back-tracking. If you forget parts of the speech, go right on. Don't

back-track, and don't look at the outline. You are trying to get the whole thought pattern in mind, so don't get entangled in details.

4. Study your outline again and note the places where you skipped parts of the speech, or got the sequence out of order. Patch up these parts mentally, then read the outline again *aloud,* slowly and thoughtfully, but still without back-tracking.   .

5. Put aside the outline and rehearse the speech aloud from start to finish, without back-tracking.

REHEARSE THE SPEECH FORMALLY FROM FIVE TO TEN TIMES, REHEARSE ON YOUR FEET AND PREFERABLY IN A LARGE ROOM

The above rehearsals were intended merely to fix the outline in your mind. Now come the rehearsals for carrying the speech out to the audience. From centuries of experience man has accumulated the knowledge on how to create a speech from thoughts-in-the-mind. This is the way:

1. *Rehearse on your feet.* You don't remember merely with your brain. You remember with your nerves and muscles also. This is often called "muscle memory," and it is essential to beginners preparing a speech. You are going to give the speech while standing up. Ergo, rehearse the speech while standing up. Then you can get the muscular set you will use in the final speech. Also, by standing up, you can pay attention to posture and action.

2. *Rehearse in a room roughly the size of the classroom.* This is not necessary for all rehearsals, although preferable, but certainly for a few rehearsals you need to stand up in a full-size room and get the feel of your voice as it comes back to you from the four walls. For this use a classroom in late afternoon or evening. Sometimes two students pair off, hold a practice session together, and criticize each other.

3. *Rehearse where you are free from interruptions.* This is so obvious that it needs no elaboration.

4. *Rehearse the speech formally from five to ten times.* The number of needed rehearsals is not fixed, and these numbers are suggestive. Few students will need less than five. Some will need more than ten. But one thing is certain: Most students need more rehearsals than they think. During the first rehearsals you are still fixing the speech in mind. The next few allow you to attend to posture

and action, and especially *poise*— that essential to all good speaking. The last rehearsals allow you to make sure that the fine shades of thought—the humor and suspense and all the other elements that make up what is known as *feeling, mood,* and *attitude*—are projected to the entire room.

CLASSIFIED SPEECH SUBJECTS

The Story of (Narrative)

Calling the Constitutional Convention	McGuffey's readers
College life in early days	Penicillin
Modern music	The surrender at Appomattox
The microscope	Henry Ford's first automobile

The Cause of (Analysis)

Detroit being the automotive center	Tornadoes
Iowa being the corn center	Juvenile delinquency
High taxes in the U. S.	High prices after wars
The American Revolution	Poe's erratic genius

A Critical Exposition of (Description)

A speaker I recently heard	Lobbies
A book I recently read	Recent U. S. foreign policy
A course I am taking	Jet plane development
The curriculum of this institution	Modern art

How It Works

The photo-electric cell	A woman's mind
Running a student paper	A county political organization
Pressure cookers	Grading beef
Radar	Offset printing

What It Is

Honor system	Reciprocal trade agreements
Farm parity prices	Medians, means, and averages
Octane rating	Bebop music
Closed shop	Realism in literature

History and Biography

Churchill's England	Life at Jamestown in 1607
Samuel Johnson's England	Stump speaking a century ago
Florence Nightingale	The San Francisco Vigilantes
Eleanor Roosevelt	The early railroads

Books, Art, Music

Bach	The real Mark Twain
Classical music	Carl Sandburg, poet and biographer
Origin of the comic strips	Zane Grey and the westerns
Al Capp as a satirist	Ivanhoe

Exercises

1. Go to hear a speaker and evaluate his extemporaneous ability:

   a. Is his speaking punctuated by breaks in fluency like these:
   "Now I—*Er*—believe that—*Er*—the true facts are. . . ."
   "I want to say—*to say*—that the best thing is. . . ."
   "The reason for this is that—*the reason is that*—we cannot. . . ."

   b. As you make a key-word outline of the speech, do you find that the speaker has wandered off the line of thought?

   c. Does he waste time and words simply because he has not packed his thoughts into concise form?

   d. In his enthusiasm or wandering does he tend to exaggerate—for example, saying *many* when he means *a few?* saying *absolutely* when he means *probably?* saying *everybody knows* in place of *some people think?*

2. Analyze one of your instructors in the manner explained in Exercise 1.

3. Prepare a 4-minute speech, following the Seven Steps set forth in this chapter. In order not to overlook or treat casually any step, use the following procedure: Make a Time Table of your speech preparation and hand it in with the outline. On it list the Seven Steps, and show when you started each one and when you completed it. This is a mechanical procedure, and is for beginners only. For them it is excellent, because it shows the source of trouble or failure in first speeches.

Chapter 4

BEING SEEN

Y ou will remember that we saw in Chapter 1 why no one can literally "deliver a speech," that what we commonly call "delivering a speech" is actually a process of *using light waves and sound waves to make listeners think what you are thinking.* In this chapter we shall consider the use of light waves, or what the listeners see.

Why Speakers Use Action

A significant thing about action is that when you ask the average listener he will say it is not important. Indeed one survey showed that only 27 per cent of the people in selected audiences thought "gesture" was essential to good speaking, and only 46 per cent thought "coordinated body movement" was essential.[1] So widespread is the misunderstanding of what is meant by "gesture" and "action" that we should pause for a survey of its place in thinking and in communication.

ACTION IS AN INHERENT PART OF THINKING

What do we think with? Only the brain? Hardly. The brain is like a telephone exchange, useless without the lines running into it from the outside. It is the switchboard, not the whole system. It receives incoming signals, makes proper connections, and sends messages through to their destination. For efficient service the body must function as a *whole.*

Where is your "mind"? Is it in the brain? Or perhaps in the nervous system? Actually we cannot say that the mind is in any particular *place.* It is not a thing, like a leg, or even the brain. It is an activity, a function. Aristotle, twenty-three centuries ago, observed that *the mind was to the body what cutting was to the ax.* When the ax

[1] W. K. Clark, "A Survey of Certain Attitudes Toward Commonly Taught Standards of Public Speaking," *Speech Monographs,* XVIII (March 1951), No. 1, 62-69.

is not in use, there is no cutting. So with the mind. "Mind," said Charles Henry Woolbert, "is what the body is doing." We don't think merely with the brain, or even with the nervous system. We think with brain, nerves, glands, and muscles, working together as a whole. A physically inert speaker is not thinking at his fullest.

Total activity is necessary for thinking. Total activity is also necessary for communicating thought from one person to another. Observe how people go about ordinary conversation. If you have never really paid attention to it, you have a surprise in store. Good conversationalists nod their heads, shake their heads, lift their eyebrows, and let change of feeling play across their faces. They bend, turn, swing, droop, and shrug their shoulders. Their hands are still hardly more than a few seconds at a time.

Now these people are not making speeches, they are simply communicating to one or to other people what is in their minds. They are not conscious of using action. They are merely human beings, talking the way human beings have talked for half a million years.

For half a million years people have talked with head, face, hands, and body. Remember that. Face frankly the fact that you cannot abolish the habits of half a million years.

VISIBLE LANGUAGE IS AN OLDER CODE OF COMMUNICATION THAN SPOKEN LANGUAGE, AND IS MORE BASIC

When Columbus discovered America he found copper-skinned natives who had been separated from peoples of the Old World for some 18,000 years. They spoke approximately 100 different word-languages, none of them related to the languages of Europe, *but these newly-discovered natives shook their heads for "no," and nodded their heads for "yes," exactly as did Columbus' crew of Mediterranean sailors, and as had the Greeks, Romans, and Egyptians. These newly-discovered natives raised their right arm to greet an approaching stranger, as had the knights of Medieval Europe. They turned palms down to express disapproval, palms up to express approval, and lifted their hands in supplication—exactly as other people did everywhere in the world.*

Visible language, sign language, is older than spoken language. It is more uniform. It is written deeper into our organism. It carries more basic meanings. We use spoken words for refined thought, but for the deep basic meanings we use action. We are civilized, yes; but *the eye is still quicker than the ear.*

You are about to give a speech. Before you utter a word, you begin to talk to all who see. Do you stand with a timid, uncertain stance, or with poise born of confidence? Do you gaze with a frozen face and a fishy eye, or does change of thought and feeling travel across your face? *Every speaker gives two speeches simultaneously, one with words, and one with action.* If both carry the same messages then you are truly communicating. But when words say one thing, and action says another, listeners usually let the words go by and gives first attention to the action. Why? Action tells them the real meaning. There they see the false smile, the evasive glance, the sickly grin, the random grimaces of confusion. There is the real speech, and listeners know it. The eye *is* quicker than the ear, and sign language *is* older than spoken language.

ACTION HOLDS ATTENTION

Did you ever lean forward, muscles tense, while watching a game? Did you ever feel your muscles contracting as if to throw a ball, make a catch, shoot a basket, or do whatever the players are doing? Whether you know it or not, you have engaged in such mimicry. It is the spectator's basis of enjoying the game.

This phenomenon is known as *empathy.* It may be defined as *feeling ourselves into* whatever we perceive. All perception, in fact, involves this participation. We not only wind up with the pitcher, swing with the batter, and plunge with the fullback, but also feel ourselves into static situations. When we see a painting or stand before a cathedral, our like or dislike hinges largely on whether the object evokes pleasant or unpleasant tensions in our bodies. We are unconscious of this participation, to be sure, as we are of our breathing or our heartbeat. But it influences our behavior profoundly.

Now apply this to the audience. *Unconsciously they imitate the speaker.* The speaker has no option whatever on whether his action will affect the audience, for it *must* affect them in one of three ways:

1. If he uses too little action, empathy in the audience will be weak. Because it is weak, the audience will not remain physically alert, but but will relax more and more into physical—and therefore mental—inaction. But the more one relaxes, the less active becomes the mind, until in complete inactivity one goes to sleep. So the speaker who uses no action puts the audience into a state too near sleep for them to follow alertly what he is saying. They will sit and half listen; but, when he is through, they will recall little of what he has said.

2. If the speaker uses distracting action, action that he never intended using and often does not know he is using, the audience will be forced into fitful and distracting responses. We have all seen the speaker who buttons his coat and then unbuttons it, or twists a handkerchief in his hands, or rocks up and down on his toes, or toys with an object on the table. "If he moves that watch again, I'll scream," whispered a woman after a speaker had put his watch in twelve or fifteen places over the table. She did not scream vocally, nor did she listen to what he was saying. She sat tense, waiting for him to move that watch! So with all people. They are distracted by empathetic response to a speaker's uncontrolled action.

3. If the speaker uses controlled action, communicative action, listeners find it easy to follow what the speaker is saying. They participate, "feel in," and give the speaker sustained attention.

"Must I use gesture?" asks the timid, or diffident, or nervous student. The frank answer is that you cannot say "No" to life. Action is part of the process of thinking. Action is a universal sign language far older than spoken words. Action arouses attention. Action is inherent in good private conversation. Add it up yourself.

Exercises

1. Prepare and give a two-minute speech on empathy. To prepare this speech, attend an athletic contest, an exciting motion picture, a circus, a vaudeville performance, or any other event where you will witness alert bodily movements. (a) Observe carefully the stresses and tensions of your own body, and (b) observe the behavior of those around you. Do you "feel in" with the performer? Is this "feeling in" revealed chiefly by leaning forward with tension? Or does it break out into the open so that the spectator tenses or relaxes, moves to right or left, with the performer?

2. Practice in your room and demonstrate in class vigorous and appropriate action on the following:

    a. "Halt! Who's there . . . Advance and be recognized!"

    b. "I mean it. I propose to stand here. Not to move, but to stand *here.*"

    c. "Will you listen, please? What else could we have done? What else did we have a *right* to do?"

Making Action Effective

Effective action hardly seems like action at all. It seems natural, spontaneous, done on the impulse. Indeed, action that calls attention to itself is bad because it distracts instead of communicates. A good speaker never seems to be "gesturing" at all. He is merely a person who makes you understand him, and who happens to use light waves as well as sound waves. Hence the adage, "Great art conceals art." There are five constituent parts of this art.

CONTROL YOUR POSTURE

No single posture is best for everyone, although some postures are bad for everybody. From the listener's standpoint, a good posture should not call attention to itself. From the speaker's standpoint, a good posture should allow ease of bodily movement, ease of breathings, and voice projection to fill the room.

Suppose we start with a good military posture. Understand that a military posture is *not* a good speaking posture. It is too stiff and formal. But we can modify it into a good speaking posture:

1. Heels together on the same line (or, for speaking, heels fairly close together).

2. Feet turned out and forming an angle of about 45 degrees.

3. Knees straight without stiffness.

4. Hips level and drawn back slightly; body erect and resting equally on hips; chest lifted; shoulders square but not lifted.

5. Arms and hands hanging naturally at the sides.

6. Head erect, chin drawn in so that the axis of the head and neck is vertical, eyes to the front and not on the ceiling or floor.

7. Weight of the body sustained partly on the balls of the feet, heels resting on the floor.

8. The entire posture to appear natural and graceful, to be without rigidness or exaggeration, and to be one from which action is possible without first relaxing muscles that have been constrained in an effort to maintain the posture.

From this fairly rigid military posture, you can develop a speaking posture that fits your individual personality and mode of speaking. Probably the one essential of good posture is to *"stand tall." To stand tall, reach up with the top of your head. Reach up with your spinal column. Reach up with your chest and abdomen. And with your legs reach down to the floor.*

You will not learn this posture from merely reading about it. So rehearse it day after day. Practice even how to *sit tall* and *walk tall.* Make it part of your speech behavior.

ADLAI STEVENSON

These candid and characteristic pictures show effective action at its best.
Each seems natural and spontaneous, hardly like action at all.

LEARN HOW TO USE A SPEAKER'S TABLE

For beginners, and for those self-made speakers out in the world at large, a speaker's table or lectern is a booby trap. Beware of it. Its function is to make the platform look less bare and to serve as resting place for a water pitcher, a vase of flowers, or the speaker's manuscript or notes. But it snares the undisciplined speaker in a myriad of ways. He uses it for a crutch. He uses it for a stanchion on which to rest his weary frame. He uses it as a shelf for paper clips, watch, and other toys to be fingered and fondled.

Probably for a beginning speaker it would be a good thing if he had no table or lectern to tempt him. If it is there, however, *stand tall behind it*. Rest your hands on it if you feel more at ease that way, but don't slump down on it, or hook your elbows on the edge of it.

TALK TO THE AUDIENCE, NOT TO YOURSELF

Until you have disciplined yourself to self-control you are likely to engage in random action: licking your lips, loosening your collar, smoothing your hair, shifting your feet, or letting your posture wilt. You may be startled to find that your hands have grown to enormous size; you cannot conceal their size from the audience, so you try to get them out of the way, behind your back, or in your pockets. These actions are symptoms of inner emotions. Unwittingly, but with deadly effect, you are telling the audiences that you have lost control of yourself. We have discussed this under stage fright, both causes and treatment (pages 20-23).

There remains a milder form of disorganized action to be discussed here, namely *self-directed gestures. This is the tendency of speakers to gesture to themselves instead of to the audience*. It takes various forms:

1. You clamp the elbows tightly against your body, and gesture toward your face.

2. You guard the stomach with your forearm, often using the hand for a weak gesture but keeping that arm-block between you and the audience.

3. Or you may reach out arms and elbows toward the audience, but keep the palms—the real carrier of meanings—turned toward your face.

Now self-directed action is not really a problem of action at all. The real cause is your mental attitude. First, you are thinking about *yourself*, not the audience. You are not speaking to help the audience, for when you start helping people you are no longer afraid of them. Further, you are not enthusiastic over what you have to say. Once you get enthusiastic, you will literally "forget yourself into good speaking."

Effective action talks to the audience, not to the speaker. But get first things first. *When your action fails to talk to the audience, the trouble is not with "gesturing." It is with your mental attitude. You cannot be afire for people to hear you—all the people, even those in the back row—without reaching out to them with action as well as with voice.*

GESTURE WITH THE WHOLE BODY

The runner does not run with his legs and feet alone, but with his whole body. The baseball pitcher does not pitch with his arm alone, but with his whole body. The speaker does not speak with his voice alone, or with his voice plus his hands. He speaks with his whole body. This is the imperative plus of communicating by physical action.

If you want to be ludicrous, make gestures without this teamwork of muscles. Whether intending to be funny or not, you will be. The actor Charles P. Sale attained his first reputation in character parts by "speaking a piece" with detached gestures. His arms and hands moved like a puppet's pulled by strings. For an added punch he would throw in, now and then, a hand movement that came a shade too soon, or too late. He was never all-in-one-piece, but gave the effect of one who had "studied gesturing" and was following the rule without the spirit.

Now suppose we put into practical operation this principle of all-in-one-piece action. Stand before a mirror and assume a good posture. Then speak the following without gesture but with total body vigor and strength:

Government *of* the *people, by* the *people*, and *for* the *people* shall not perish from the earth.

The action involves every part of your body: hand, arm, shoulder, head, torso, leg, knee, ankle, and foot. The action is *built into* the whole-body action, and is not "something added on."

Now try it again, emphasizing the words *of, by* and *for* by any type of hand action—putting the whole body behind it all-in-one piece.

Try it still again, using (1) the right arm, (2) the left arm, (3) both arms.

Effective action should point, indicate, suggest, separate, emphasize—carry some particular *definite* meaning.

Definite hand action involves three phases: the *approach*, the *stroke*, and the *return*.

The *approach* is the "get ready" movement. It is like raising a gun to take aim. You make this approach well ahead of time and you hold it until you are ready for the emphatic stroke.

The *stroke* carries the meaning. It is like pulling the trigger. If you are going to emphasize that "The time is *now*," the approach may have been started even before the first word of the sentence is spoken. Your body is set for action, beforehand, and on the word *now* comes the stroke—backed by the whole body all-in-one-piece.

The *return* is the "as you were." After you have held the idea before the audience long enough for them to see it fully (don't hurry it, and don't backlash your gestures), you simply let the hand fall to the side in its original position. Avoid bringing it back in a wide curve. Just let it fall naturally, without fanfare or tick-tocking.

Kinds of Action

Perhaps it will help you to consider three specific kinds of action that every speaker uses: platform movement, basic hand action, and action of the head and face.

PLATFORM MOVEMENT

Movement on the platform is not essentially different from movement anywhere else. But a speaker is like a fish in a glass bowl. He is before everybody's eyes, and everything he does is magnified. On the platform avoid two extremes, the extreme of standing stock-still through the whole speech, and the extreme of pacing like a caged animal. Total lack of movement tends to lose audience interest. Too much movement tends to distract attention.

In general, effective platform movement is made forward and backward, instead of from side to side. Side-to-side movement often signifies only nervousness. Forward and backward movement, on the other hand, is part of the half-million-year-old visible code. People step closer to others, or lean toward them, when they are deeply in earnest or want to be especially emphatic. Speakers do the same thing.

Backward movements, though not necessary, are useful at times to indicate divisions of thought. They are like chapter headings or paragraph indentations in print. In effect they say to listeners, "I now come to a new part of the subject."

This homely advice may seem unnecessary. It may seem like saying what everybody knows. But speakers on the platform are under nervous tension. This tension tends to find outlet in aimless wandering, until it becomes a habit. Habit is a powerful force. You had best get it on your side. What you do in practice you will likely do later in performance. Therefore, from the start, practice controlled posture and movement.

BASIC HAND ACTION

The following six kinds of hand action are a universal sign language, older in the human race than words, and understood by people regardless of whatever word-language they use:

1. *Locating.* You point to an idea or a thing. "A hundred years ago," you say—as you point behind you to indicate that you are speaking of the past. "Tomorrow," you say—as you point forward to indicate the future. "This idea," "that principle," "yonder map," "at the right," "on the left," "before us,"—all such things are pointed out for the eye of the listener. In a sense they *see* what you are talking about.

2. *Dividing.* You have a series of ideas or facts, and you want to keep them separate in the listeners' minds. Therefore, you use dividing action. "On the one hand liberals say . . . ," while with the palm held vertically you put the liberals on your left. "On the other hand, conservatives say . . . ," while with the same action you put the conservatives on your right. In the same way" this *vs.* that," or "first, second, third," are divided by the hand into separate parts. In print you divide ideas with subtitles and paragraph indentations. In speech, you use dividing action.

3. *Describing.* This type of action suggests the shape, size, or movement of things. "It was this long," you say—and measure the distance with both hands. "It was round,"—and with both hands you round it out. In the same way you indicate movement. "It winds through a valley"—and you trace its winding with a finger.

4. *Approving.* More than any other, this is the gesture of friendly relation, of exchange, of giving and receiving. It is made with an open hand gesture, palm upward, held out as though to give something or to receive something. With this action you carry such ideas as, "This I do believe," or "Here is a duty we cannot escape," or "I present this for your consideration."

5. *Rejecting.* Off the platform, when people are not self-conscious, this is a common action. On the platform, most students find it difficult. This probably is because they are afflicted at least mildly by self-directed, body-guarding gestures. They cannot reject and body-guard, both at the same time; but the nervous tension that causes body-guarding is deep and fundamental, so rejecting action is blocked from their public platform behavior. What is rejecting action? It is simply the normal action any person makes in pushing away something he does not like. A baby makes it spurning food. An adult makes it in pushing away a dog with muddy paws. It is made with the palms down, or away from the speaker. With this action you say, "I don't like it," or "I distrust it," or "That's not the way."

6. *Emphasizing.* When a speaker wishes to lift a word or phrase or sentence above the level of context, he gives it emphasis. Behind the emphasis of voice he may also throw emphasis of action— an index finger, a hand thrust forward or downward, or even the clenched fist. Emphasizing action would be used to carry the following thoughts:

> "You ask, 'What is our aim?' I can answer in one word: 'Victory'— victory at all costs, victory in spite of all terror."

> "Don't join the book-burners!"

THE HEAD AND FACE

The head and face are the most commonly used and among the most effective instruments of gesture. By a nod of the head we indicate approval; by a shake, disapproval. Eyelids open in joy, surprise, amazement, or wonder; they contract in anger, envy, or concentration; they sparkle with happiness, or glitter in wrath. Lips may curve into a smile, or curl in contempt; they may be pulled down in a frown, or pursed into a determined straight line. Good conversationalists communicate that way in private speech. Good speakers do it in public speech.

Exercises

1. Study the action of a poor speaker: preacher, politician, teacher, fellow student, or anyone who is invariably dull:

   a. Study this speaker's muscular tone. Does his posture suggest muscular or mental alertness? Does it suggest inertness or flabbiness? Does it suggest rigidity or tension? Does he gesture with the whole body all-in-one-piece? If not, which parts were not used? Did his action "talk to the audience," or "talk to himself"? Was it definite?

   b. Study the empathy of the audience. Do most of them follow the speaker with an alert eye? Do any appear to be drowsy? Do some avoid looking at the speaker?

   c. Write a paper on your assessment of the speaker's action and the audience's response.

2. Do the same thing with a notably good speaker.

3. Practice the following exercises in your room and be ready if necessary to repeat them in class. Follow these directions:

   a. Use *spontaneous* action, not planned action. Pay no attention to rules, elegance, or correctness, but act on impulse.

   b. Use *abundant* action; avoid restrained or half-hearted movements.

   c. Use the *whole body*, all-in-one-piece.

   d. First try simply to express your thought and feeling. Later repeat the exercise in front of a mirror and observe how it would look to others.

      1) "I looked out the window. We were flying at 2,000 feet, and there was New York coming slowly toward us. The Statue of Liberty passed by on our left, looking small as a ten-cent toy. Steamships below us moved like bugs that walk on the water. Ahead were the skyscrapers. But from the air they didn't scrape the sky. They were only toys made to imitate the real skyscrapers you see from the streets. From the air, all New York was a toy-land and I felt like Gulliver landing in Lilliput."

      2) "How ill this taper burns! Ha! who comes here?
      I think it is the weakness of my eyes
      That shapes this monstrous apparition.
      It comes upon me. Art thou any thing?
      Art thou some god, some angel, or some devil,
      That mak'st my blood cold, and my hair to stare?—
      Speak to me what thou art."

                                                            SHAKESPEARE

4. In your room practice the following kinds of action until you get the feeling behind them; then demonstrate your mastery in class:

  a. Getting the *whole* body into all action.

  b. Using the *approach, stroke,* and *return* in hand action.

  c. Freeing the wrist so that action will not seem wooden.

  d. Getting the hand *open* instead of leaving the fingers curled and awry.

  e. Turning the palm toward the audience.

  f. Using *both* hands, instead of one only as beginners tend to do.

5. Study the following paragraph until you have it word-perfect. Then, using the types of action you practiced in Exercise 3, communicate this paragraph by words and action:

> Nor must a young man compare himself with others or measure his success by theirs. It makes no difference how other men succeed. Their success is theirs; not yours. It matters nothing to me that Edison can invent the electric light and I can't; that Kipling can write a "Recessional" and I can't; that you can plead the law and I can't. You can do one thing; I try to do another. But success is for both of us just so far as we do well what we can do. Every man is himself, and it is in proportion as he gets out of himself the power there is within him that he succeeds—succeeds in doing the thing he is best fitted to do.
>
> EDWARD BOK

6. The following selection is more conversational. Try reading it and reinforcing your words with communicative action:

> As Mr. John Oakhurst, gambler, stepped into the main street of Poker Flat on the morning of the 23rd of November, 1850, he was conscious of a change in its moral atmosphere since the preceding night. Two or three men, conversing earnestly together, ceased as he approached, and exchanged significant glances. There was a Sabbath lull in the air, which, in a settlement unused to Sabbath influences, looked ominous.
>
> Mr. Oakhurst's calm, handsome face betrayed small concern in these indications. Whether he was conscious of any predisposing cause was another question. "I reckon they're after somebody," he reflected; "likely it's me." He returned to his pocket the handkerchief with which he had been whipping away the red dust of Poker Flat from his neat boots, and quietly discharged his mind of any further conjecture.
>
> In point of fact, Poker Flat was "after somebody." It had lately suffered the loss of several thousand dollars, two valuable horses, and a prominent citizen.
>
> BRET HARTE

Chapter 5

BEING HEARD AND
UNDERSTOOD

Wᵉ now come to the use of *sound waves* in communicating thought. "Anybody can talk," runs a thoughtless adage; but talking is not necessarily communicating. Some people talk with voices that are weak and thin. Some have lingual inertia and immobile lips. Some do not open the mouth; they only half-open it. Some do not actually carve the sounds of speech; they only approximate them. To say that such people talk is a liberal extension of the meaning of that word. More exactly they mumble, drone, mutter, muffle, sputter, haw, and croak. We are concerned here with talk that communicates. Public address is *enlarged* conversation, and the enlarging gives trouble. It starts with the nature of hearing itself.

The Nature of Hearing

Hearing in public address is done at greater distance and under more adverse conditions than in private conversation. The nature of hearing, therefore, enters the picture. Let us look at how the ear operates.

When the sound waves arrive at the ear they must, first, be translated into thought in the listener's mind. Now what we call sound waves are really *pressure* waves. The pressure waves of the faintest audible tone at the most favorable pitch move the ear drum in and out by less than a hundred-millionth of an inch. When this movement reaches the inner ear it contacts an auditory nerve which has some 30,000 fibers. These fibers are the pathway through which the dot-dot-dot code of nerve impulses reach the brain and are translated into thought. This inner ear is the sound analyzer. Among its chief means of analysis are these:

1. *By energy of sound.* The louder the tone, the greater is the number of nerve fibers stimulated. Also the louder the tone, the more impulses pass along each fiber per second. Thus the speaker who uses greater energy increases the total number of nerve impulses delivered to the listener's brain in two ways: (1) More fibers are active, and (2) more impulses are sent per fiber. Here we see why a weak voice in a large room is not enough, and why a full voice communicates more meaning.

2. *By rhythm.* Each language has a characteristic rhythm determined partly by its grammar and partly by its pronunciation. Hence a stilted or artificial speech rhythm hinders understanding.

3. *By stress and accent.* Certain melody patterns are standardized, and the ear is conditioned to translate them. So it is that by timing of syllables, and by pause between them, the ear translates additional meanings. So it is that monotonous voices, lacking stress and accent, give the ear fewer impulses to translate.

4. *By pitch.* The inner ear sorts out the various frequencies in each complex sound. Each frequency stimulates a corresponding group of the 30,000 nerve fibers. Stimulation of certain fibers causes us to hear a high pitched tone, and stimulation of others causes us to hear a low-pitched tone. To use an analogy, "hearing a high-pitched tone corresponds to feeling a touch on the face, and a low-pitched tone to a touch on the foot." [1]

So "hearing others talk" is far from simple. Even in a quiet living room we do not hear as much as we think. Continually we are filling-in, guessing at sounds, and even words, that we don't quite hear. Listening at greater distance and in greater noise compels us to guess more and fill-in more. Research on intelligibility, therefore, found that "increasingly higher levels of intelligibility are required in the friendly conversation, the classroom with a small class, the classroom with a large group, and the public platform and stage." [2]

Being Heard

To be understood you must first be heard. To be heard in public address requires certain specific disciplines.

[1] Hallowell Davis, *Hearing and Deafness* (New York: Murray Hill Books, Inc., 1947), p. 47.

[2] William B. McCoard, "Contribution from the Military Programs in Voice Communications," *Quarterly Journal of Speech*, XXXIII (October, 1947), 370.

SUPPLY VOCAL POWER FROM BELOW THE LARYNX

A public speaker needs energy enough to be heard easily, and energy enough to carry tone color and informing inflections. Here you face two difficulties. First, some people try to get power by constricting the muscles in the throat and neck; the result is sounds that are harsh, shrill, or brittle. Second, some try to speak without adequate energy; and the result is lifeless tones without salt and spirit.

Power of voice comes from pressure behind the breath stream. This pressure, in turn, comes from muscles in the abdomen and between the ribs. In the words of the old Victorian actors, you *"pack your tones against your belt."* Lift the front wall of the chest. Harden the abdomen. Pull down the diaphragm until it draws air into the lungs like a suction pump. Now you can "pack your tones against your belt." Further steps are these:

Maintain a steady air pressure as you talk. In good voices there is steady muscle action in exhaling. In poor voices it tends to be jerky. Steadiness, of course, does not mean uniform pressure. You increase the pressure for emphasis and accent. You vary the graduation according to the thought. But the pressure is not wavering or jerky, not booming forth at the start of a sentence, then fading to inaudibility at the end.

Maintain an adequate breath reserve. You do not keep your lungs filled to the last cubic inch, or else you soon will have a chest full of air with burned out oxygen. Instead, you take a reasonably deep breath and fill the chest comfortably. In the same way, you do not keep on talking until you run out of air, but refill smoothly with short catches of breath. This ample reserve enables you to maintain vigor of voice to the end of each thought.

Exercises

1. Practice breathing. Stand erect. Pull down the diaphragm and draw air into the lungs. While inhaling also: (1) Lift the upper chest. (2) Push out the ribs. (3) Harden the abdomen. (4) Try to feel the muscle-pull in the small of the back. (5) Make sure the throat is *open and relaxed.* Now exhale without a sound by letting the air flow silently through the lips.

2. Stand erect and inhale as above. Then with relaxed and open throat, speak the following with maximum energy and prolonged tones:

> *All aboard!*
> *Forward! March!*

3. Stand erect and inhale until the chest is comfortably filled. Then speak the following with maximum vocal power. Keep the throat relaxed. Supply power from below. Sustain the stressed sounds:

> Hear the mellow wedding bells—
> Golden bells!
> What a world of happiness their harmony foretells!
>
> EDGAR ALLAN POE, *The Bells*

> The bell invites me.
> Hear it not, Duncan; for it is a knell
> That summons thee to heaven or to hell.
>
> SHAKESPEARE, *Macbeth*

USE AMPLE RESONANCE

The vibrating vocal cords in your larynx produce only a thin and feeble tone. You must amplify and enrich this tone with the resonators. What are the human resonators? You have two types, fixed and adjustable. The *fixed resonators* are unchangeable in size: the skull bones, nose, nasal sinuses, trachea, sternum and ribs. When you use any of them you get the feeling of resonance in that part of your body. Close the lips and hum *m-m-m-m* until you get this feeling. Then put your hand on top of your head and you will know whence comes that "feeling." It is the real thing, for your skull bones are vibrating! Also feel the chest. If you are using enough energy down in your bellows, the chest bones are also vibrating.

Adjustable resonators are those that can be changed in size, shape, and tenseness: the mouth, pharynx, and larynx. These adjustable resonators change the pitch of your voice. They give it the rising and falling inflections. They impart the subtle variations of vocal quality. Especially they give it the vowel quality, for by changing the size and shape, and tension of these adjustable resonators you can turn one sound into *e*, another into *o*, still another into *i*. You use about 15 vowel sounds. To produce each one clean and clear requires a different size, shape and tension of the adjustable resonators.

Some people use their resonators efficiently; and we say they have "good voices." Some don't; and they have poor voices of various degrees and types.

Exercises

1. Inhale (remember your breathing exercises), relax the throat, flatten the tongue and make the sounds given below. Hold the tone for 15 seconds

PRESIDENT FRANKLIN D. ROOSEVELT

His normal key was high, a distinctly tenor voice. His voice was flexible and responsive, with subtle informing inflections.

Acme

SIR WINSTON CHURCHILL

His lisp was no handicap. It was lost in his overtones of subtle thought and rich double meanings.

United Press

while you feel the cranium, jaw, chest, etc., and locate which of these resonators are vibrating. Note that the mouth must be *opened wider* for each succeeding pair:

e and oo
a and o
i and ah

2. Read the following with relaxed and open throat, and the power coming from bellows down below:

I have but one lamp by which my feet are guided, and that is the lamp of experience.

PATRICK HENRY

There are maidens in Scotland more lovely by far,
That would gladly be bride to Young Lochinvar.

SIR WALTER SCOTT

Ship me somewhere east of Suez, where the best is like the worst,
Where there aren't no Ten Commandments, an' a man can raise a thirst.

RUDYARD KIPLING

USE YOUR NORMAL KEY

Your voice has a normal key. This is the general pitch level best suited to your particular resonators. Your voice will rise and fall above and below this median, but it tends always to return to it.

The normal key varies with different persons, and it varies greatly between men and women. In this respect voices are like musical instruments. Each will produce sounds within a given range, some high, some medium, some low. Outside this range it does not perform so well. Hence some women's voices are contralto, and others are soprano. Some men's voices are bass, and others are tenor.

If you do not use your normal key, you cannot attain best potential voice power or quality. If you speak below it, you tend to have a deep hollow tone without flexibility. If you speak above it, you tend to have a thin squeaky voice, with the same lack of flexibility.

The best way to find your normal key is to sing from your lowest key to your highest, including your falsetto. Your normal key is about *one-fourth* the way up from your lowest tone.

Exercises

1. Using the method described above, find your normal key. By going frequently to a piano and sounding the proper key, you can keep this pitch continually in mind and help to make its use habitual.

2. Using your normal key, read the following, but do not read in a mono-pitch. Instead communicate the meaning by as much variety of pitch as you need, but use your normal key as the median:

> We hold these truths to be self-evident, that all men are created equal, that they are endowed by their Creator with certain unalienable Rights, that among these are Life, Liberty and the pursuit of Happiness.
>
> *Declaration of Independence*

> Friends, Romans, countrymen, lend me your ears;
> I come to bury Caesar, not to praise him.
> The evil that men do lives after them;
> The good is oft interred with their bones;
> So let it be with Caesar.
>
> SHAKESPEARE, *Julius Caesar*

Being Understood

Being heard does not mean that automatically you will be understood. We may hear words in a foreign language, or indistinct sounds in our own language, and understand them only partly or not at all. Let us look at how to be understood in enlarged conversation.

SPEAK WITH A FLEXIBLE AND RESPONSIVE VOICE

The inner ear, you remember, is the sound analyzer. It takes in the sound waves, translates them into nerve impulses, and sends them to the brain along selected groups of the 30,000 fibers of the auditory nerve. But it cannot analyze what is not there. You must supply the material. The more you supply, the more analysis there is and the more meaning. The human race, in fact, has evolved a code of meaning from changes in pitch, time, and emphasis—a code that is independent of the words themselves. Its use is as involuntary as the twinkle of the eye.

COMMUNICATING MEANINGS BY CHANGES IN PITCH

We communicate meanings by two kinds of pitch changes: *steps* and *slides* (i.e. inflections). The Step is a pitch change *between* sylla-bles, as seen in the following sentence:

```
                    he
                        do?
        What
            did
```

The *Slide* (inflection) is even more common, and is used constantly for communicating subtle shades of thought. It is a gliding pitch change *during* the syllable, as in saying sarcastically:

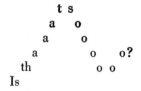

```
                    t s
                  a   o
                a     o
              a         o   o?
            th            o o
          Is
```

For thousands of years these pitch changes have been used to communicate meanings. Each person will have his own personalized variations, but the standard meanings are far older than any words of the English language and quite as definite:

a. *A rising inflection communicates incompleteness of thought, uncertainty, or inconclusiveness.* When you ask a question, hesitate, or are in doubt, or cannot make up your mind—your voice says so with a rising inflection.

       / / /   /
    Are you leaving us?   (I want to know.)

    / / / /   / /
    To be or not to be   (I am not sure about this.)

b. *A falling inflection communicates completeness of thought, assurance, conviction, or determination.* This is the inflection of decision and assurance. It is used less often than rising inflections, but carries more definite and important meanings.

    \   / / / \
    This I do believe   (And believe it earnestly.)

    / /   /   /   \ / /   \
    I will not retreat a single *inch!*   (Nothing shall move me.)

c. *A wave, or double inflection, communicates the rich double meanings of humor, sarcasm, and subtle thought.* Not all thought is plain and straight. Often we really say two things at once. Such meanings are communicated by a voice wave, or double inflection. In other words, when there is a double thought in the mind, there is a double inflection in the voice.

/ ∧
Oh Yeah?   (Don't expect me to believe that!)

/   / ∧   ∨
Yes, I suppose so.   (But I am not sure.)

/   /   / / ∧   ∧
For Brutus is an honorable man.   (Honorable outwardly, but
                                        a traitor within.)

Bare words, in short, mean little. They are given fullness of mean-ing by subtle shadings of voice. The word "no," said Charles H. Woolbert, can be spoken to carry at least twenty different meanings, one of them being "yes."

In public address the special problem is to enlarge the inflection to fit the enlarged conversation. The short inflection, suitable enough for ordinary conversation, is not enough for the enlarged conversation of public address.

Exercises

1. Read the following to communicate the question-and-answer current of ideas:

> Does the road wind up-hill all the way?
>   Yes, to the very end.
> Will the day's journey take the whole day long?
>   From morn to night, my friend.
> But is there for the night a resting-place?
>   A roof for when the slow dark hours begin.
> May not the darkness hide it from my face?
>   You cannot miss that inn.
> Shall I meet other wayfarers at night?
>   Those who have gone before.
>   CHRISTINA ROSSETTI, *Up-Hill*

COMMUNICATE MEANINGS BY VARIATIONS IN TIME

We don't speak at a constant rate like a steady wind blowing. We change the rate, pause, and group our words. These time variations are part of man's code of communicating.

a. *Rate.* Some people think fast and talk fast. Some think and talk at a slower tempo. Webster, for example, spoke at about 80-100 words a minute, Lincoln at 100, Franklin D. Roosevelt at 117, Henry Clay at 130-160, John C. Calhoun at 180, Rufus Choate at 200, and

Phillips Brooks at 215. Each talked according to his own personality and his capacity for clear articulation. If you talk too fast, the sounds become obscure. If you talk too slow, you tend to have blank pauses, or to fill in time with *Ahs* and *Ers*. In general a rate over 150 words a minute is too fast, and if you slow to 100 words a minute, there is danger of the audience's losing interest—unless you have exceptional syllable duration and use especially effective pauses.

All this applies to the *average rate*. Actually, we do not speak long at an even rate. When dealing with narrative, suspense, or excitement, we speed up to fit the mood. When explaining or moving through a difficult thought, we slow down markedly. To sum it up: *Talk fast enough to be interesting. Take time to be distinct to those who are farthest away*.

b. *Word Grouping*. We don't talk in single words, but in groups of words. We group words together, according to the meaning. One word group, for example, may carry the central meaning of a thought and the others merely fill in details. If we change the grouping, the identical words may have exactly the opposite meaning, to wit:

> The teacher said the student is a fool.
> "The teacher," / said the student, / "is a fool."

The essence of grouping for clear meaning is this: *Group together those words which stand for ideas that belong together, and separate that group from others by emphasis and pauses*.

The essential of effective word grouping is the *pause*. In speech you don't have commas, semicolons, and periods. You have the pause. It is the punctuation mark of speech—the comma, semicolon, and period all rolled into one. A pause permits listeners to concentrate on what has been said and get set for what is to come. A pause is that "thunder of white silence" that causes restless listeners to look at the speaker, and to listen sharply. "I . . . made a pause," said Winston Churchill, "to allow the House to take [it] in. . . . As this soaked in, there was something like a gasp."

Beginners seldom know how to pause. They are afraid of the silence, like a child of the dark. They hurry on to fill it up with talk and rush on to that final blessed word. This is not real speaking. It is a race with time. Therefore, take stock of yourself. Do you group words firmly enough? Do you pause positively? Can you listen to the silence of your pauses, and allow listeners this moment of golden silence to digest what you have said and to get set for what is to come?

Our final word. Beware of pausing at every place you find a punctuation mark in print. Pausing and punctuation often fall at the same place, but not always. Punctuation is for the eye. Pausing is for the ear. For the eye punctuation is like this:

> Let us, therefore, brace ourselves to our duties, and so bear ourselves that, if the British Empire and its Commonwealth last for a thousand years, men will still say, "This was their finest hour."

But for the ear, pauses come at five places where there is punctuation, at three additional places where there is no punctuation. Furthermore, there are no pauses at two places where there is punctuation:

> Let us, therefore, / brace ourselves to our duties, / and so bear ourselves / that, if the British Empire and its Commonwealth / last for a thousand years, / men will still say, /"This / was their finest hour." /

Exercises

1. Which of the following would you read at a faster rate, and which slower. In succession read the two at rates that seem best for you:

> Out of the North the wild news came,
> Far flashing on its wings of flame,
> Swift as the boreal light which flies
> At midnight through the startled skies.
> And there was tumult in the air,
>   The fife's shrill note, the drum's loud beat,
> And through the wide land everywhere
>   The answering tread of hurrying feet.
>   T. B. READ, *The Revolutionary Uprising*

> The Moving Finger writes; and, having writ,
> Moves on; nor all your Piety nor Wit
>   Shall lure it back to cancel half a Line,
> Nor shall your tears wash out a Word of it.
>   OMAR KHAYYÁM, *Rubiayat*

2. Pause forcibly with packed meaning to communicate full meaning on the following:

> Books are the best of things, well used; abused, among the worst.

> He batted his eyes, and the lightnings flashed;
> He clapped his hands, and the thunders rolled.

COMMUNICATING MEANINGS BY DEGREES OF EMPHASIS

We don't emphasize each word equally. If we did human speech would resemble the *tap, tap, tap* of a typewriter. But speech is not like that at all. It comes in bursts and swells.

In each sentence a single idea dominates, and this idea often is conveyed in a single word—with all the other words being mere undercover support. In speaking we highlight the important idea-carrying words by emphasis, and let the others fade into the background:

> I tell you *earnestly* and *authoritatively* you must get into the habit of looking *intensely* at words, and assuring yourself on their *meaning, syllable* by *syllable*—nay, *letter* by *letter*.

In public speaking emphasis is far stronger than in private conversation. This, in part, is because the audience is composed of persons of various degrees of intelligence and alertness, and it is necessary to reach all—including the dullest. Again, speaker-to-audience distance is a factor. The farther away a speaker is, the harder it becomes to read his facial expression and other minute signs of meaning, and the more the audience must depend on the speaker's distant voice and on action that cannot be seen close up. In short, *enlarged conversation demands enlarged emphasis.*

Exercises

1. Read the following so as to bring out the full force of the neat insult:

> Sir, I admit your genial rule,
> That every poet is a fool,
> But you yourself may serve to show it,
> That every fool is not a poet.
>
>   ALEXANDER POPE

2. In the following speech on "The American Scholar," Emerson attacks the traditional higher education of over a century ago. His style is condensed and it will require full emphasis to communicate the meaning. Read it as to an audience of one hundred people.

> Books are the best of things, well used; abused, among the worst. . . . The book, the college, the school or art, the institution of any kind, stop with some past utterance of genius. This is good, they say—let us hold by this. They pin me down. They look backward and not forward. But genius looks forward: the eyes of man are set in his forehead, not in his hindhead: man hopes: genius creates.
>
>   RALPH WALDO EMERSON

3. The thought in the following passage rises and falls like rolling ocean waves. Read it so as to communicate all the rising and falling, but keeping the thought rolling on to its splendid climax:

> You ask, "What is our policy?" I will say, "It is to wage war, by sea, land, and air, with all our might and wealth against a monstrous tyranny, never surpassed in the dark, lamentable catalogue of human crime. That is

our policy." You ask, "What is our aim?" I can answer in one word:
"Victory"—victory at all costs, victory in spite of all terror, victory, however long and hard the road may be; for without victory there is no survival. . . . But I take up my task with buoyancy and hope. I feel sure that
our cause will not be suffered to fail among men. I feel entitled to claim
the aid of all, and I say, "Come, then, let us go forward together with our
united strength."

WINSTON CHURCHILL, *On Becoming Prime Minister*

COMMUNICATING MEANINGS BY DISTINCTNESS OF ARTICULATION

The average speaker talks at a rate of about 300 syllables a minute,
or 5 per second. A listener must catch these syllables on the wing and
translate them into thought. He must do it instantly, without faltering
and almost without pausing. But if these 5-syllables-a-second are
slurred, muffled, or projected weakly the listener is going to miss some
of them. If, at that moment, he stops to think, "What was that he
said?" then he misses also those words that come in the instant of
thinking back. All in all, he has missed a whole section of what the
speaker said. So it is that in public address clear articulation is vital
to communication.

By articulation, of course, we mean the skillful molding of speech
sounds, and the combining of separate sounds to make up intelligible
speech. Loudness of speech is mainly in the vowels, but *intelligibility
is mainly in the consonants.* Hence the maxim, "the vowels give
beauty, the consonants give clarity." Unfortunately, consonant sounds
are not loud even at close range; and, unfortunately also, they fade
with distance, so that a consonant sound heard easily at 5 feet may be
inaudible at 50 feet. Hence to be heard easily in public address you
must sharpen the articulation of consonants. The following tested procedures will be helpful:

a. *Pack plenty of breath pressure behind the consonants.* Explode
the initial *p* as in *pull, t* as in *talk,* and *k*-sound as in *chemist.* Use
ample breath pressure to sound the medial consonants like the *zh*-sound
in *measure,* the *sh*-sound in *nation,* and the *s*-sound in *recent.* Carry
this breath pressure all the way through to the final consonants; explode the *t* in *don't,* hiss the *s* in *miss,* prolong the *l* in *control.* It takes
far more breath to project consonants than to vibrate resonant vowels.
Shallow breathers take note.

b. *Articulate; don't slur, mumble, or muffle.* People who really
articulate open their mouths wide. They have an active jaw, lips, face,

tongue, and pharynx. Ironically, not only can you hear good articulation but you can look at the speaker and also see it. There is the constant nimble movement as the visible speech organs move into position for the consonant, make the sound, and speed swiftly on to the next one. Here are two broad and convenient self-made tests:

First, look at yourself in the mirror as you talk. Do you see the swift and nimble movements that come from the strength of contact and quickness of release of the visible articulating organs?

Second, listen to your voice, both as you speak and from recording playbacks. Do you say *What's that* or *whassat? Let me* or *lemme? Don't know* or *dunno? Recognize* or *reckernize? Particular* or *partikerler? Manufacture* or *manerfacture?*

c. *Sustain the friction-like consonants:* the *s* in *sit* and *hiss*, the *z*-sound in *his*, the *sh*-sound in *motion*, the *zh*-sound in *occasion*, the *f* in *half* and *four*, the *v* in *never* and *move*. These sounds are made by partially blocking the breath stream at some place in the mouth and by forcing out the breath at this place in a *continuous* stream. Make the stream continuous.

d. *Hold the long consonants until you get them rolling:* the *l* in *hill*, the *r* in *road*, the *n* in *now*, the *m* in *home*, and the *ng* in *coming*. These are sounds that require a build-up. Therefore, build them up.

e. *Do not ignore medial consonants.* Which do you say: "twen*t*y," or "twe*nn*y"? "Star*t*ed," or "star*d*ed"? Do you have the clear medial consonants in ro*st*rum, hu*nd*red, e*xt*ra, di*sp*rove?

f. *Sound the final consonants in a word group.* When combinations of consonants occur within a word group, we blend them, as in "the fair bree*z*e *bl*ew, the whi*te* *f*oam *fl*ew." But when a consonant sound falls at the end of a word group, it needs to be carried through and articulated with full breath pressure:

> Nights candles are burnt ou*t*, / and jocund day
> stands tiptoe / on the misty mountain top*s*. /

g. *Master the difficult consonant combinations.* The English language is infamous for its many difficult consonant combinations. There are 22 two-consonant groups that number far over 100 individual combinations. Beyond that are 58 reasonably common three-consonant and four-consonant combinations. The following list is helpful. Practice it, being careful to articulate all of the consonants without slurring or omitting any within the combinations:

TWO-CONSONANT COMBINATION[3]

outside	bracelet	robbed	looked	past	month
number	noiseless	lived	pushed	ask	brings
insect	almost	pulls	waked	myths	help
dismal	million	raised	songs	bulb	feeds

THREE-CONSONANT AND FOUR-CONSONANT COMBINATIONS[4]

explain	aptly	fixed	next	hinged	posts
misquote	exactly	asked	acts	asks	guests
discreet	directly	commenced	judged	desks	eighths
language	mostly	lunched	edged	tests	months

Exercises

1. Pronounce the above word lists to a friend. Have him sit at right angles to you or with his back turned, so he cannot see you but must depend wholly on sound. Ask him to write down the words slurred or weakly articulated. Remember that these are not mere words that give you trouble; they are *sound combinations*. Note the combinations. (They are italicized in the above word lists.) Make up a list of words containing these sounds for future practice.

2. If possible make a recording of these word lists and listen to them yourself.

3. Pronounce the following pairs of words so that listeners can easily distinguish one word from the other:

pear	bear
toe	dough
fine	vine
what	watt
hiss	his
rich	ridge

4. Drill on the following words until you can pronounce them without slurring or omitting any of the sounds:

WRONG	RIGHT	WRONG	RIGHT
kep	kept	monts	months
exackly	exactly	aw-right	all right
coss	costs	wader	water
insiss	insists	unided	united
raerroad	railroad	ass	asks

[3] Remember that letters and sounds are not identical. Thus in the second column "bracelet" is pronounced with the sound of *sl*, "noiseless" is pronounced *zl*. Observe that in the fourth column "waked," etc., are pronounced with a final *t*, not with *d*. Finally, do not be disturbed that words like "month" and "brings" are spelled with three final consonant letters. They have only two-consonant sounds, since *th* and *ng* are single sounds.

[4] Note that the words in column 3, although spelled *ed*, are pronounced *t*.

5. Read the following and be careful not only of articulation but also of communicating the mood and rich double meanings:

> There was once a little man, and his rod and line he took,
> For he said, "I'll go a-fishing in the neighboring brook."
> And it chanced a little maiden was walking out that day,
>   And they met—in the usual way.
>   ANON., *The Usual Way*

> Maris is simple and chaste—
>   She's pretty and tender and modest—
> But on one or two matters of taste
>   Her views are distinctly the oddest.
> Her virtue is something sublime—
>   No kissing—on that there's a stopper—
> When I try, she says, "All in good time—
>   At present it's highly improper."
>   GILBERT AND SULLIVAN, *Haste to the Wedding*

We are spinning our own fates, good or evil, never to be undone. Every smallest stroke of virtue or vice leaves its never-so-little scar. The drunken Rip Van Winkle, in Jefferson's play, excuses himself for every fresh dereliction by saying, "I won't count this time!" Well, he may not count it, and a kind Heaven may not count it; but it is being counted none the less. Down among his nerve-cells and fibers the molecules are counting it, registering and storing it up to be used against him when the next temptation comes. Nothing we ever do is, in strict scientific literalness, wiped out.

                                   WILLIAM JAMES, *Talks to Teachers*

MAKE YOUR VOICE THE VEHICLE OF THOUGHT AND FEELING

This is the final goal of all voice training. Everything else in this chapter has been on the ways and means to prepare for it. A good voice carries to listeners your finest degrees of thought, and slight shade of values, every color and hue.

Foremost of all things your voice should tell is *sincerity*. To all who hear, it should say, "You may disagree with what I say, but you cannot question my sincerity." No listener, of course, really knows whether a speaker is sincere. He can know only whether a speaker *seems* sincere. "Say what you think," William Jennings Bryan used to say to his daughter, "but *feel* what you say." Now sincerity is not easily feigned. The surest way, the only safe way, to sound sincere is to *be* sincere.

Once you have established sincerity, then comes the meaning of the words themselves. Remember that when you speak or read you communicate *two* simultaneous meanings. First, you say, "This is what I am talking about." Second, you say, "Here is how I feel about it." Like the two legs of the human body, both are essential.

There is no absolute meaning any word must have. The dictionary establishes only a frame of reference by recording many meanings for almost every word. At the moment of utterance you give each word its exact meaning in context. You spot the important words, let listeners know they are important and why, and communicate their meanings with precision—as *you* use them. You go below the surface of language and make clear your basic thought. This is not done by the mere utterance of words, for the mere flow of words may confuse the listener if their exact meaning and their relation to the whole thought are not made clear.

Finally, you tell listeners, "This is how I feel about these things." This is done by what we call *emotional color*. You have been using emotional color, and hearing others use it, all your life without probably knowing the term. Listen to a good speaker, and you know unerringly whether he feels determination, anger, contempt, friendship, or indifference. Each attitude is communicated by its own special tone color. The tone color of each is distinct from others, arrogance from assurance, friendship from flattery, mirth from melancholy.

How do you make voice the vehicle of thought and feeling? Shall you say, " I shall emphasize this word," or "Here I want to show determination; therefore, I shall use the emotional color of a determined person?" Not if you want to be a real speaker. If you do this, the result will be like that described (in this case a bit unjustly) by a critic of Olivia de Havilland: "She never seems to feel the part—only the importance of it. She never seems in love with Romeo—only with *Romeo and Juliet*. She recites poetry where she should radiate it; and goes through the role as though following a score marked presto or lento, *ff.* or *pp.*" Listeners know whether a speaker feels what he says, or is only feigning. This is old knowledge in the human race, learned early in every life.

If you soliloquize, your voice will be a soliloquy. If you only half-grasp the thought, your voice will be perfunctory. To communicate thought you must be *thinking* on your feet, creating or recreating the full thought at the moment of utterance. To communicate attitudes you must *experience* the attitude as you speak. "Expression," said Cicero, "is always perfect." To make voice the vehicle of thought and feeling, you must think in terms of ideas, feelings, and concepts instead of mere words.

Exercises

1. Study the following selection, get its central theme and supporting details, then in reading it communicate the full meaning:

One comfort is that great men taken up in any way are profitable company. We can not look, however imperfectly, upon a great man without gaining something by it. He is the living fountain of life, which it is pleasant to be near. On any terms whatsoever you will not grudge to wander in his neighborhood for a while.

THOMAS CARLYLE

2. What is the dominant mood of the following selection? Is it reverence, loyalty, admiration, entreaty, command, coaxing, anxiety, remorse, or gratitude? Decide which you think it is, and read it to communicate that mood:

And Ruth said, Entreat me not to leave thee, and to return from following after thee; for whither thou goest, I will go; and where thou lodgest, I will lodge; thy people shall be my people, and thy God my God; where thou diest, will I die, and there will I be buried: Jehovah so do to me, and more also, if aught but death part thee and me.

Book of Ruth, 1:16-17

3. In reading the following selection communicate its humor and suspense:

There was an old preacher once who told some boys of the Bible lesson he was going to read in the morning. The boys, finding the place, glued together the connecting pages. The next morning he read on the bottom of one page: "When Noah was one hundred and twenty years old he took unto himself a wife, who was"—then turning the page—"one hundred and forty cubits long, forty cubits wide, built of gopher-wood, and covered with pitch inside and out." He was naturally puzzled at this. He read it again, verified it, and then said: "My friends, this is the first time I ever met this in the Bible, but I accept it as an evidence of the assertion that we are fearfully and wonderfully made."

HENRY W. GRADY

4. In the following communicate the undercurrent of uneasiness:

Once upon a midnight dreary, while I pondered, weak and weary,
Over many a quaint and curious volume of forgotten lore,—
While I nodded, nearly napping, suddenly there came a tapping,
As of someone gently rapping, rapping at my chamber door.
" 'Tis some visitor," I muttered, "tapping at my chamber door:
Only this and nothing more!"

EDGAR ALLAN POE, *The Raven*

5. Study the meaning and determine the mood of the following selections. Then read them to communicate both meaning and mood:

> I recollect a nurse called Ann,
>> Who carried me about the grass,
> And one fine day a fine young man
>> Came up, and kissed the pretty lass;
> She did not make the least objection!
>> Thinks I, "Aha!
>> When I can talk, I'll tell Mama."
>> —And that's my earliest recollection.

FREDERICK LOCKER-LAMPSON, A Terrible Infant

> In Flanders fields the poppies grow
> Between the crosses, row on row,
> That mark our place; and in the sky
> The larks, still bravely singing, fly,
> Scarce heard amidst the guns below.

JOHN D. McRAE, In Flanders Fields

Chapter 6

ORGANIZING THE SPEECH INTO CONCISE AND ORDERLY FORM

In a well-planned speech the ideas are presented "as organized platoons— in marching order." How to organize them and how to make them march—these are problems we shall now consider.

Select a Definite Purpose

A speaker, like a traveler, ought to know where he is going. He ought to plan in advance how to get there, find out what detours and blocked roads, if any, there are along the way. Then when the speech is finished, no one in the audience will be asking, "Where was he trying to go?" They will know.

This may seem like unnecessary advice, but experience warns otherwise. Many people make speeches without object or aim, and you have heard them. They start nowhere. They go nowhere. They aim at nothing—and succeed perfectly in hitting nothing. Therefore, when you plan a speech, find out where you want to go, and keep on the road.

THE FOUR GENERAL PURPOSES OF SPEAKING

What possible purposes may a speaker have? Fundamentally, there is but one basic purpose of all speaking. The speaker wants his audience to *respond, to do something about what he says.* But not all responses are equally easy to attain. Some are easier, some are more difficult. Hence they are here divided into four groups, arranged according to increasing difficulty:

TO INTEREST THE AUDIENCE

What shall it profit a speaker if, no matter how good the speech, the audience is uninterested and pays no attention? Obviously the stream of interest must run through *all* speaking. The "polite attention" which courteous members of the audience may give for a while will not last, nor will it be very close attention, for the more energy spent by the hearer in "giving attention" to the speech, the less energy will be left to understand and consider the subject matter. Interest, then, is the common denominator of all speaking.

There are times, however, when interest is not the means, but the end itself. At such times the speaker does not want to inform, to stimulate or to convince the audience. He wants only to interest them. He deals in wit, repartee, stories, and dramatic movement. He relaxes his hearers and takes their thoughts from the tension of everyday cares.

Such is the purpose of most private conversation, of a toastmaster's introductions, of "filling-in" speeches at meetings or organizations, of much after-dinner speaking, and of story-hour talks for children.

TO INFORM THE AUDIENCE

Next is the speech to inform. Typical of these are reports, group instruction to workers, classroom lectures, and lectures given by specialists to the lay public.

The purpose of such speeches is to tell people something they don't already know. This is a more difficult speech than the speech to interest, for the information needs presenting so that listeners can grasp, understand, and use it. It is never enough that the speaker merely pass out the information. He must see that the listeners get it in usable shape. The following points are to be borne in mind:

1. *Arrange the information under two or three topics, not more than four at the most.* A speech cannot be strung out like the links of a long chain. Listeners simply cannot remember such scattered information. Take all your facts and group them under a few main topics. If possible, two topics are best perhaps. Three are all right. But, if you have more than three, be careful. Listeners are likely to forget them.

2. *In giving the speech, fasten these topics in the listeners' minds.* When you come to the first topic, say so. Tell listeners, for example, *"The first step in this problem is. . . ."* When you get through with

that topic, tell them you are through, and summarize it so they will remember. Then, as you take up the second topic, let them know that it is the second one: *"We now come to the second problem. . . ."*

3. *Always make your information specific, never abstract.* This does not mean for you to clutter the speech with needless facts and figures or confusing decimals, but it does mean for you to be specific, to give details, to illustrate and compare. For example, you would not say, "The distance was 199 miles and 4,039 feet." for the listener might remember the 39 feet—which is unimportant—and forget the 199 miles, which is the essential figure. Better say, "The distance was slightly under 200 miles," and so fix the essential figure in the listeners' minds.

4. *Use charts, graphs, and diagrams if the material is technical or complex.* The eye sees proportions more easily than the ear can follow explanations about them. A tabulation of assets and liabilities makes their explanation simple; the design of a building can be quickly shown by a sketch; the operation of a machine can be better explained by a diagram. Arrange your material so listeners can see as they hear, and complex information is made easier to explain.

5. *Make your information interesting.* Remember that people who listen are just plain human beings. They can take in so much, and no more. After that, all facts begin to look the same to them. So use anecdotes and illustrations along the way. Make interesting comparisons. Add humor to give your facts flavor.

TO STIMULATE THE AUDIENCE

We now come to the more difficult levels of response, the two levels found in persuasive speaking.

What is persuasion? Obviously, it consists of vitalizing a proposition so as to make it a dynamic force in the thinking and action of other people. But people have many levels of beliefs. Some beliefs are shallow, temporary, subject to easy change. Some are deep-rooted and hard to change. The listeners' level of belief determines the speaker's mode of approach. For convenience we here divide them into two levels. First are beliefs we hold in a mild form. Second are those we hold tenaciously and sometimes obstinately.

Speeches to stimulate are concerned only with the first kind, where belief is accepted only in a mild form, or where lip-service is given

A UNITED NATIONS CONFERENCE IN GENEVA

The delegates visible in this picture speak 19 different languages. The language barrier is overcome by linguists who translate each speaker's words over the headphone system.

*to the proposition but where the listener fails to practice it in the
actual conduct of life.*[1]

We may, for example, believe that we ought to study our lessons,
get eight hours of sleep each night, obey traffic laws, and take an
active interest in public affairs—yet our belief may be too mild to
impel vigorous conduct. Likewise, we have many other near-beliefs
that influence our behavior very little or not at all.

Most public speaking aims at vitalizing these mild beliefs. Among
such speeches are most sermons, most political addresses, commencement addresses, inaugural addresses, dedications, pep talks in
college, inspirational talks to businessmen, addresses at reunions,
and addresses at celebrations. The speaker's object is to *stimulate*
listeners into an active dynamic acceptance of mild beliefs, or to
stimulate them to action on propositions to which they agree, give
lip-service, but do nothing about.

A speech to stimulate is more difficult than a speech to interest or
to inform. Interest it must have, and information also, but it must
have more. It must also consider the wants, hopes, and aspirations of
the listeners. It must set up what H. B. Gislason has aptly called "an
adequate system of rewards" for those who accept the speaker's
proposition. It must *motivate* the proposition—fasten it into the
listeners' wants, hopes, and aspirations—until it becomes vitalized
in their thinking and conduct.

TO CONVINCE THE AUDIENCE

*Here the speaker is dealing with propositions that are not accepted
by the listeners, or are outright disputed by them. He is asking for
the listener to alter his opinions, to vote, to join, to do, to give, to go.
He may be asking listeners to "believe this thing earnestly," or to
"do this thing actively." The first is action of the mind. The second
is action of the body. Both are action.*

To convince is the aim of the lawyer who defends a client, the
legislator who argues for a bill, of the spokesman who asks you to
support the new federal policy on business or agriculture, of the

[1] Let us be sure to understand the meaning of *stimulate* It is here used in the literal
sense given by *Webster's New International Dictionary*, second edition: "to excite, rouse,
or animate, to action *or more vigorous exertion* by some pungent motive or by persuasion." Other writers have used the word *impress* to designate this purpose. But,
literally, *impress* means to stamp or imprint something, and so implies that the speaker
merely stamps or imprints an idea on the inert mind of the listener. In contrast, the view
here taken is that the listener never merely has an idea imprinted in his mind, but that
he *participates actively*, like a player catching a baseball. Hence we use the more appropriate word *stimulate*.

speaker who presents the view that vital literature is as essential to society as material techniques.

To convince is the most difficult of all speech purposes, because it commonly includes all the other three. There must usually be interest, information, and stimulation, but also something more. There is added the burden arising from dealing with propositions that must be *proved true*, with proof acceptable to the knowledge, prejudices, and wants of the listener. Ordinarily only after this proof is acceptable to the listener can the speaker vitalize the subject, make it dynamic, and motivate the listener's behavior.

Let us summarize the speech purposes. (1) All speeches have one fundamental purpose of gaining a response. (2) But some responses are harder to win than others; therefore they are divided into four groups, known as General Purposes, and are arranged according to increasing difficulty:

1. To Interest	+	
2. To Inform	+ +	
3. To Stimulate	+ + +	
4. To Convince	+ + + +	

PHRASING THE PURPOSE-SENTENCE

After selecting your controlling purpose, you then frame it into a single, simple Purpose-Sentence. A good Purpose-Sentence has two distinguishing qualities. First, it states the central idea in plain words. It is the proposition you want to develop, to amplify, to make rich with meaning. It is the proposition you want listeners to accept after you have given it full coverage. Put it in a simple sentence, without circling around the idea, and without backing into it:

POOR: It is important that people should not believe all that they read in print, because today much that is written is propaganda.
(*This circles around the idea, getting tangled in too many words.*)

GOOD: Learn to read suspiciously.

POOR: To have continued prosperity in the U.S. it is necessary for this country to be able to sell goods in foreign countries.
(*Again circles around the idea; again tangled in too many words.*)

GOOD: The U.S. needs foreign markets.

Next, a good Purpose-Sentence is best stated in terms of the response you want from listeners. By stating it this way you are less likely to try the impossible, and more likely to limit yourself to a response you can actually get. You cannot, for example, persuade die-hard Democrats or Republicans to change parties, but you have a fair chance to persuade them that the country is better off if they soften hostility to the party in power. So in phrasing the Purpose-Sentence you ask: "How far can I lead them in my direction?" In one speech you can lead only so far. If you attempt too much, the speech will backfire. Here is an example:

> POOR: The people who criticize modern education are screwballs who want to return to the horse-and-buggy days.
> *(Those who disagree will say "Away with you!")*

> BETTER: You may not agree with critics of modern education, but you can profit from understanding their viewpoint.

A final word: You don't often state the Purpose-Sentence, in so many words, to the listeners. Certainly you will not make a didactic statement of it at the beginning. The Purpose-Sentence is not for the audience per se. It is rather for you, the speaker, to focus your thinking, and to guide your selection of materials. It is your governing idea, the goal toward which you want to lead the listeners, step by step.

Divide the Speech Into Well-chosen Main Heads

If you examine closely the structure of well-organized speeches, you will find that the central idea is supported, or in some way developed, by a very few main heads or topics. In other words, the speaker does not present the central idea in one large lump, but he breaks it into several easily-handled parts.

If you read a hundred, or a thousand, well-organized speeches, you will find that the long speeches have no more main heads than the short ones. They simply have more facts, illustrations, specific instances, and other forms of support.

To be specific, in both long and short speeches there will be found usually *two or three main heads, occasionally four or five, almost never more than five.* So uniformly will these numbers appear in speech after speech, that you would soon wonder if there were not underlying reasons. You would be right. There are definite reasons.

For obvious reason there would not be less than two main heads in a speech. Every speech, as we know, has one central idea (phrased into a Purpose-Sentence). Hence the main heads are those two or more divisions that develop, elaborate or support the Purpose-Sentence. So there will be at least two, possibly more.

You may ask: But why have *only* two or three main heads, and almost never more than five? For two reasons: (1) A speech with too many main heads lacks a thought pattern. It is arranged hit-and-miss. Any idea, if carefully analyzed, can be reduced to very few basic parts, usually two or three. (2) Listeners cannot remember too many main heads. If a speech has two or three, well-chosen and well-supported, listeners can carry them away in their heads. But if a speech has seven or eight, listeners are hopelessly confused. Therefor, arrange your material into an *obvious* thought pattern with *few* main heads.

There are five possible thought patterns for arranging main heads:

TIME ORDER

You begin at a given date or period of history and move forward (or backward) with time. The divisions are marked by the clock or calendar. For example:

The American Mind in American Literature

I. From the earliest settlements until early in the 19th century literature represented the distilled influence of American geography on European ideas, known as the Colonial Mind.

II. By 1830 American frontier optimism had given impetus to the belief in liberty and the natural goodness of man, and hence to the triumph of the American Romantic Movement.

III. After 1870 economic disillusion led the way to a critical appraisal of contemporary life, known as Realism, which has continued into the 20th century.

SPACE ORDER

You arrange material according to any pattern of space—east-to-west, near-to-far, top-to-bottom, inside-to-outside. Especially is this pattern useful for description or simple exposition. Witness Victor Hugo's famous description of the battle of Waterloo:

PURPOSE-SENTENCE: To form a clear idea of the battle of Waterloo, imagine a capital "A" laid on the ground.

I. The left stroke of the "A" is the Nivelles road.
      A. The left-hand lower point is Hougomont.
      B. Rielle is there with Jerome Bonaparte.

II. The right stroke of the "A" is the Genappe road.
> A. The right-hand lower point is la Belle Alliance.
> B. Napoleon is there.

III. The cross of the "A" is Mont Saint Jean; Wellington is there.

CLASSIFICATION ORDER

You classify topics according to some systematic division. There are many forms of classification, of which the following are typical:

1. *Classification according to fields of inquiry:*
> Economic
> Political
> Social
> Educational
> Religious

2. *Classification according to the parties involved:*
> Men and women
> Young and old
> Producers and consumers
> Labor and management

3. *Classification according to cause, as:*
> a. The primary cause was. . . .
> b. The contributing causes were. . . .
> c. The precipitating causes were. . . .

Other miscellaneous forms of classification include the following:
4. Plants and animals
5. Function and structure
6. Public and private
7. Prose and poetry

CAUSE-AND-EFFECT ORDER

You arrange material according to causes and results. You seek to determine causes by asking, "What events, factors, or circumstances caused—or partly caused—this result?" You seek to determine the kinds of causes by asking, "Which were primary causes? Which were contributing causes? Which were immediate causes?" You also seek to forecast results by asking, "What events, factors, or circumstances will result (or have resulted) from this given situation?"

Beware of False Causes. Don't mistake that which merely *precedes* for that which actually *caused*. This is an old error for which the Romans had a name: *Post hoc, ergo propter hoc.* "After this, therefore on account of this." It is also as new as this morning's bread, for gullible people still say, "This happened first, and that happened next; therefore this caused that." Beware of it. Find out which are really causes and which are mere accidents of time.

The Cause-and-Effect order is not always (1) cause and (2) effect. Often it is reversed and becomes (1) effect and (2) cause. Indeed the latter form is the more commonly used by skillful speakers. The following is an outline of Effect-Cause order in which the speaker seeks to establish real cause instead of mere time sequence:

War Causes Inflation

EFFECT: I. Inflation has accompanied every major war in U.S. History.
      A. The U.S. Department of Labor has compiled a wholesale index of prices, which shows that during the American Revolution prices jumped from 60 to 180.
      B. During the War of 1812 it jumped from 100 to 150.
      C. During the Civil War it jumped from 62 to 136.
      D. During World War I it jumped from 70 to 156.
      E. During and after World War II it jumped from 80 to 170.
      F. At no other times in the past 200 years have prices jumped so sharply except during and immediately following war.

CAUSE: II. The cause goes back to Adam Smith's law of supply and demand. . . .

PROBLEM-SOLUTION ORDER

You diagnose the problem and attempt to find a way to relieve it. But mark well that when you attempt problem-solving the route is tortuous and is trapped with pitfalls—no matter in what area you operate. Dr. Charles H. Mayo of the famous medical clinic was once asked what type of illness most of his patients had. He replied, "Mistaken diagnosis." Social, political, and economic ills suffer from the same malady: mistaken diagnosis. To avoid mistaken diagnosis analyze your problem in this manner:

1. What are the effects, nature, or external manifestations of this problem? Classify them specifically and carefully.

2. On the basis of this classification of the effects, nature, external manifestations—what seem to be the causes?

In other words, in problem-solving you first analyze the problem by using the effect-cause method just previously discussed. "Before a problem can be attacked effectively it must be stated with reasonable clarity," said Wendell Johnson. "And as soon as it has been so

stated, some kind of solution to it becomes more or less apparent.
. . . Certainly any scientific worker of experience knows that by far
the most important step toward the solution of a laboratory problem
lies in stating the problem in such a way as to suggest a fruitful
attack on it. Once that is accomplished, any ordinary assistant can
usually turn the cranks and read the dials." [2]

In social, political, and economic questions the solutions are more
complicated than this statement might indicate, but the key still lies
in the discovery and clear statement of the problem. When this is
done you can then consider the four master questions involved in
problem-solving:

1. Is there a "felt difficulty" that makes a change necessary or desirable?
   (You have already covered this, and are ready for the next three questions.)
2. Would the change I advocate remedy the situation?
3. Might it not bring on new evils worse than the present ones?
4. Would not some other solution be more satisfactory?

Or, as Raymond F. Howes aptly put it, you might ask for sake of
vividness:

1. Is the man sick?
2. Will our medicine cure him?
3. Will it harm him?
4. Will any other medicine be more effective?

Of course you will not automatically convert each of these steps
into a main head. Never would your final heads turn out to be: I.
Problem; II. Solution; III. Refuting the dangers of new and worse
evils; IV. Refuting other solutions. These are rather the *steps of
inquiry* by which you seek (1) to analyze the nature of the problem,
(2) test the various avenues of solution or escape, (3) and present
the description and endorsement of the chosen way. The following is
an example of a Problem-Solution thought pattern that presents a
two-step solution:

PROBLEM: I. The tendency to glorify the common mind, typified by the
               hero worship of athletes and glamor girls, is a positive
               danger to American Democracy.

SOLUTION: II. The challenge to higher education is to rouse interest in the
               uncommon mind.

[2] Wendell Johnson, *People in Quandaries* (New York: Harper and Brothers, 1946), p.16.

SOLUTION: III. Institutions that meet this challenge to put intellect above
                  brawn and glamor, will have rough sailing but will perform
                  a vital service.

Beware of patent-medicine remedies. Student speeches are too
much filled with them: "Here is the problem. Here is my sure-fire
cure-all." But sure-fire cure-alls are usually nostrums, dealt in especially by quack medicine makers and quack speakers. In real life we
actually "solve" few problems. Through the centuries we have never
"solved" the problems of marriage, divorce, crime, taxes, war,
tolerance, and equal justice under the law. Instead, we *keep at solving
them*. In real life, sometimes the only solutions open to us are to
"Watch this problem carefully," or "Act with courage," or "Have
faith," or "Make these few adjustments." At times even the President
and the Congress can advise us only of the general direction we
should take in solving pressing public questions. At such times it is
bad taste, not to say bad thinking, which leads a college student to
supply the cure-all in a five minute speech. It brings to mind Winston
Churchill's apt retort to free-lance advisers: "It is easy to give advice
if you have not got to carry it out."

Arrange the Entire Speech Into an Outline

 Why make an outline? Because an outline is a blueprint for the
 speech. It sets down the thought pattern in plain view, and enables
you to test the analysis and the order of arrangement. It shows at a
glance your supporting materials, whether you have the right kinds
and have enough. "The thing that distresses me most in listening to
sermons," said Bishop Gerald Kennedy to theological students, "is
the vast number of preachers who have not learned to make the most
simple outline. More sermons crack up on this hidden reef. . . than
any other. . . . An extended discourse must have a skeleton." [3]
For students an outline has another value. It is a diagnostic aid
to the instructor. From hearing the speech, then examining the outline, the instructor can tell whether a problem arose from faulty
planning or from imperfect execution.
Following are the steps in composing a good outline:

 1. *Prefix to the outline a clear and complete Purpose-Sentence.*
This serves to pin-point your purpose and to guide your selection of
materials.

[3] *His Word Through Preaching* (New York: Harper and Brothers, 1947), p. 48.

2. Organize the outline into three parts: the beginning, the body, and the ending. Ordinarily these are known as Introduction, Discussion, and Conclusion.

Introduction

I. _____

II. _____

Discussion

I. _____

II. _____

III. _____

Conclusion

I. _____

3. Number each part of the outline (Introduction, Discussion, Conclusion) as a separate unit. The entrance and exit should not be confused with the thought pattern of the discussion. Thus if you have two parts in the Introduction, the first main head (Discussion) is numbered I, not III.

Introduction

I. _____

II. _____

Discussion

I. _____

II. _____

III. _____

Conclusion

I. _____

4. Use a consistent set of symbols to indicate main heads and each descending order of subheads. From generations of usage the symbols below have become almost common law. To avoid being misunder-stood probably you had best follow general usage:

I. Roman numerals used for main heads.
  A. Capital letters used for 1st level of subheads.
    1. Arabic numbers used for 2nd level of subheads.
      a. Small letters used for 3rd level of subheads.
        (1) Parenthetical arabic numbers used for the 4th level.
          (a) Parenthetical small letters used for the 5th level.

5. *Show the relationship of headings also by proper indentation.*

WRONG

I. Every symbol ought to stand alone in the open, easily visible to the eye; this one is partly concealed by the word underneath I.
   A. Likewise this subhead symbol is partly concealed by being absorbed into the line beneath.

RIGHT

I. Note how this symbol stands alone and is instantly visible to the eye.
   A. Likewise this subhead symbol is instantly visible because it stands apart and to the left.

6. *Use complete sentences only.* This for two reasons: (1) Catch phrases are perfectly all right for experienced speakers (though relatively few use them), but you are *learning,* and in learning you need to think through each idea and to phrase it into exact words. (2) Your outline is also to help the instructor diagnose your individual problems. A catch-phrase outline is a poor diagnostic aid.

7. *Write down each main head in a simple sentence, usually with an active verb; beware of winding sentences and dangling clauses.*

POOR

I. It is because of the fact that we do not know how serious were the crises that people faced in other generations that we underrate the relative seriousness of the crises of this generation with those of the past. (*Winding and dangling!*)

GOOD

I. Every generation faces crises, and each says, "My crisis is the worst ever."

8. *Include the supporting materials in the outline.* An outline that contains only assertions—with no illustrations, factual information, comparisons, testimony, etc.,—is just about worthless. It is a skeleton without blood, organs, or life. Better use the paper for doodling. Study how each of the speeches outlined below is enriched by supporting material, pages 90 and 94.

9. *Beware of trying to support any head by one subhead; use two or more.* You really can't *divide* an idea into one subhead. Division implies two or more parts.

WRONG

I. You don't study merely by sitting at a desk.
   A. A parade of daydreams may fill your mind.
      1. Daydreaming is easier than studying.

RIGHT

I. You don't study merely by sitting at a desk.

A. Suppose you clear your desk of *Esquire* and *Life*, and the letter from home—then sit down to study, "Making the Outline."
B. In the next half hour a parade of ideas marches through your head.
   a. Your girl from home gets on your mind; "What's she up to now?" you wonder for the fifteenth time.
   b. "What about next week-end?" you wonder.
   c. "Those confounded exams, only three weeks away," you think.
C. In short, you have not been studying at all; you have been playing mental hop-skip-and-jump.

10. *Phrase each statement as you would speak it to the audience.* An outline is a runway for your takeoff into the speech. You don't want to have to change sentence structure as you take off.

WRONG
   a. Here I will tell them an experience I had last year.
RIGHT
   a. Last year I met a reporter just back from Europe, and asked him. . . .

SPECIMEN OUTLINE

The following is an outline of an eight-minute speech. The outline contains slightly more than half the number of words of the final speech:

"BY VOTE OF THE PEOPLE"

PURPOSE-SENTENCE: You had best participate in politics, lest we have an unhealthy government.

Introduction

I. Over half a century ago the Democrats in this county put on a torch-light parade for William Jennings Bryan.
   A. The Democratic newspaper next day boasted that the parade was so long that it took three hours to pass a given point.
   B. The Republican newspaper the following day replied, "Yes, it took three hours to pass a given point, *but that point was Mulhollen's saloon!*"

THOUGHT PATTERN:
CAUSE-EFFECT ORDER
Main head set in brackets because it was not stated at the beginning, but was unfolded gradually.

Discussion

I. [I charge that not enough people participate in politics.]
   A. The significant fact is not that the Democrats may have strayed from the appointed line of march, but that people in that day

took part in politics more than they do today.

    1. Arthur T. Vanderbilt, former president of the American Bar Association, says that the American government is "the government nobody knows," because citizens take no interest in it.

    2. "Why should they?" the cynic asks, "What does it matter?"

    3. It matters because the people are now working 3½ months each year to earn enough to pay for federal, state, and local taxes.

B. Yet the history of elections shows that fewer people vote today than a half century ago.

    1. Half a century ago 80 per cent of the nation's eligible voters went to the polls.

    2. Five years ago it was 51 per cent, and last year it was 57 per cent.

    3. Three years ago, in the state elections, only 40 per cent voted.

    4. In the primaries the record was even worse; three years ago only 23 per cent in this state voted.

II. We are paying for this neglect.

A. First, we are paying in corrupt officials.

    1. Not long ago, the Mayor of our Capital City, while in office, was sent to the state prison.

    2. Not long before that, a Governor, while in office, was sent to the federal penitentiary.

    3. Right after that, another Governor pleaded the Statute of Limitation to escape justice.

    4. You remember these men and these events.

B. Second, we are paying through undesirables in office.

    1. Not long ago you could not sell this state government a bag of cement, a lump of coal, or a gallon of gasoline

without "seeing the right people," and
you know what people I mean.

    2. Think how much business can be *forced*
to pay, else they be cut off from this
market!

C. We are paying because the people allow
these things to go on.

    1. My home is in Hendricks County, which
from time immemorial has been over-
whelmingly Republican.

        a. In 100 years we have elected only
two Democratic judges.

        b. Back in 1936, Alfred Landon carried
Maine, Vermont—and Hendricks
County!

    2. On the poll books of that county are
enough registered Democrats to win the
county elections.

        a. But they don't vote.

        b. So it's just punishment for them to
live under a county Republican administration.

    3. In large cities this makes government an
easy prey for political machines.

        a. In some large cities only 20 per cent
of the people vote in city elections.

        b. Hence a candidate can be elected by
a mere shade over 10 per cent—and
any well-oiled political machine can
deliver 10 per cent of the votes.

        c. Remember the Irishman who was
elected Alderman; he rushed home
and shouted to his wife, "Maggie,
I've been elected Alderman"; Maggie
gasped, "Honestly?" to which the old
boy replied, "Aw, Maggie, why did
you have to bring *that* up?"

III. We can pay even more; others before us have
done just that.

A. Some of you heard Willis J. Ballinger lecture here last year, the man who wrote *By
Vote of the People.*

    1. In this book he told of the old democ-
racies—Athens, Florence, Venice—who

degenerated, not by civil war and violence, but by small groups effecting
changes.

2. The majority became indifferent; they
concerned themselves with money-mak-
ing and culture; and small groups ef-
fected the change "by vote of the
people."

B. Judged by that standard, how healthy is
this nation today?

Conclusion

I. Perhaps I ought to add the weight of two former Presidents.

A. Said Herbert Hoover: "A splendid storehouse of integrity and freedom has been
bequeathed to us by our forefathers. In
this day of confusion, of peril to liberty
our high duty is to see that this storehouse
is not robbed of its contents."

B. Said Franklin D. Roosevelt: "We have a
rendezvous with destiny."

II. But what destiny? By vote of the people, we
shall decide.

BACK-CHECK THE OUTLINE WITH A TECHNICAL PLOT

Inherent weaknesses in a speech can be seen in the outline, but they
are not always obvious to the inexperienced. By means of a Technical
Plot, however, hidden weaknesses are brought to light.

To test a speech in this way, leave ample margin on the left of the
outline, a margin of perhaps two or three inches. In this space set
down *what you are doing in the outline*. Where you have used an illustration in the outline, write "illustration" in the left column.
Where you have used testimony, humor, or tried to build suspense,
you write "testimony," "humor," and "suspense."

When this is done you can test each part of the outline. Have you
used enough facts or figures, or have you relied too much on assertion? Have you overworked pure dull explanation? Do you need testimony? Such weaknesses can be discovered by a Technical Plot.

The following outline for a six-minute speech contains 80 per cent
of the words of the final speech. Its Technical Plot shows that the
speaker's main supporting materials are specific instances, testimony,
illustration, and restatement.

HOW TO STUDY

Technical Plot *(What the speaker is doing)*	*Outline* *(What the speaker is saying)*
	PURPOSE-SENTENCES: Studying, thinking, and remembering go hand in hand, so that the absence of one leads to the loss of all three.

Introduction

I. In selecting a subject for this Monday morning's speech, I had to consider the heavy week-end we've all had.

II. I anticipated that talking to you would be like talking to a wall; I anticipated also that every word I spoke would vibrate my fragile head; therefore I chose a subject that would keep us both awake, a subject that, with final exams coming up next week, becomes more important every day; my subject is *how to study*.

III. William James once said that, "The art of remembering is the art of thinking," and I propose to show that studying, thinking, and remembering all go hand-in-hand, so that the absence of one leads to the loss of all three.

THOUGHT PATTERN:
CLASSIFICATION ORDER

Discussion

I. In order to study you must think.

Assertion

Assertion
A. The fact that we are conscious is not proof that we are thinking.

Hypothetical illustration
1. We may take a train ride and at the end of the ride say to ourselves, "I've been thinking."
2. In truth, you probably have not thought for a single minute.

Assertion
B. Actually, you think only when you are faced with a problem.

Hypothetical illustration
1. If your train had suddenly lurched to a stop with screaming brakes, you would have started thinking, "Is there danger?" and "How can I escape?" because you faced a problem that was immediate and urgent.

Restatement
2. But if you were faced with no problem on your train ride, you probably would not think.
   a. You would look at people's faces.

	b. You would admire, or deprecate, their clothes, figure, and form.
Assertion	C. The process is the same with formal study.
Specific instances	1. You clear your desk of *Esquire, Look,* and the letter from home—then sit down to study, "How to organize a speech into concise and orderly form."
Assertion	2. In the next half hour a parade of ideas marches through your head.
Specific instance	a. You wonder about that assignment in Math.
Specific instance	b. Your girl in Ohio gets on your mind again; "What's she up to now?" you wonder for the fifteenth time.
Specific instance	c. "What about next week-end?" you wonder.
Specific instance	d. "Those confounded exams, only a week away!" you think.
Specific instance	3. Also, and naturally, you talked with a couple of other people who happened by.
Summary; and climax	4. In short, you have not been studying at all; you have been playing mental hop-skip-and-jump.
Assertion	5. This is the *normal* way the mind and body behaves; both are restless.
Assertion	a. The human body is restless.
Specific instance	(1) I'm restless as I give this speech.
Specific instance	(2) You're restless as you listen to it.
Specific instance	(3) Even at night you turn over from 20 to 45 times while you are asleep.
Assertion	b. The human mind is quite as restless as the body.
Testimony	(1) Attention comes in "spurts" and we can think of nothing longer "than a few seconds at a time"; this is testimony of psychologists from Walter Dill Scott to John Frederick Dashiell.
Testimony	(2) What we call prolonged attention is, they say, simply "repeated spurts of attention" on the same subject.
Testimony	(3) William James once said that the only difference between his

mind and any poor mind was that he could keep his spurts of attention from getting off the subject.

Transition

(So when we study, our problem is to keep our repeated spurts of attention focussed on the subject, and to do this we must narrow our thoughts to the point where the problem, or point in question, is in view.)

Assertion

II. First, we should attend to the physical aspects of study.

Assertion

   A. Clean up your study area of all probable sources of interruption.

      1. Have a definite place to study, and at that place do *nothing else* but study.

Specific instance

         a. Don't write letters there.

Specific instance

         b. Don't play cards there.

      2. Avoid disturbances.

Specific instance

         a. Pictures on your desk or nearby wall can distract you.

Specific instance

         b. A turned-on radio is certain to distract you; that popular notion that you can study while listening to a radio is wishful thinking.

      3. Above all, don't get too comfortable.

Restatement

         a. Over-comfort is good for *sleeping*, but not studying.

Restatement

         b. A good idea is to lean forward and put your elbows on the desk.

Assertion

   B. Follow a definite study program.

      1. Review the previous lesson first.

Restatement

         a. This will put you in the mood to study.

Restatement

         b. It will also give you something to tack your new lesson to.

      2. Look at the *whole* lesson before you begin, so you can relate each part to the whole.

      3. Underlining the book is a good idea, but a better one is to *write* in your own words on the margin, or to *outline* it in your notebook.

      4. Finally, recitation is a great help to learning.

Restatement

         a. Recite it to yourself a few times.

Restatement

       b. The more times an idea enters your head, the better it sticks.

Assertion

III. Next, we should observe the mental aspects of study.

Assertion

A. Study with the *intent to remember*, not just to pass an exam.

Figures

    1. Extensive experiments show that it is possible to remember from 20 per cent more to 400 per cent more simply because of the intent.

Factual information

    2. These experiments showed that those who studied to pass an exam, forgot when the exam was over; those who studied to remember kept on remembering when the exam was over.

Assertion
Illustration

B. Immediately apply to life what you study.

    1. Harry Overstreet gives a significant illustration of this; he asked a philosophy student studying Spinoza to go to Coney Island and see what philosophy he could find there; the student stared in astonishment, for respectable Ph.D. candidates did not do that sort of thing, they got philosophy out of books.

    2. This man had not learned to apply his knowledge to life.

Assertion

C. Try to develop and maintain your interest in the subject.

Restatement

    1. When you tire of one subject, switch to the study of another.

Restatement

    2. If you have no interest in a subject, you will be less likely to remember it.

Assertion
Restatement

D. Find a good reason for studying a subject.

    1. A good reason gives you a *motive* for remembering.

Illustration

    2. Everybody knows the story of the boy who was dull in physics until he learned one day that physics explained why airplanes flew and what made radio work; and after that he had little trouble remembering physics.

Conclusion

Summary

I. If you get nothing else from this speech, get these three points: (1) Clear your study area: (2) retain your interest in the subject: and (3) apply your knowledge to life.

Humor
II. Follow these rules, my lords and ladies, and I'll guarantee that you'll know and understand your freshman English by the time you leave graduate school.

Exercises

1. Use the following steps in outlining a magazine article:
   a. First, determine the central idea, then phrase it into a Purpose-Sentence.
   b. Next, study the thought movement and development until the main divisions become clear; then write these out as main heads.
   c. Finally, in subhead form set down the supporting material.

2. Go to hear a speaker and make a detailed key-word outline of the speech while he is giving it. Then go home and write out the full outline, together with a critical evaluation:
   a. Did the speech have a definite purpose? If so, was it stated in plain words, or only implied? Where in the speech was this done?
   b. Did the speech have definite main heads? If so, were they stated clearly? Were they arranged in a clear thought pattern?
   c. Was there enough supporting material? Was it the right kind of material?
   d. If *you* were giving this speech how would you change the outline?

3. For one speech round make a key-word outline of each speech as it is being delivered, and later fill out enough details so you can remember the content. At the end of the round, submit a list of the two best-outlined and the two worst-outlined speeches. Give your reasons.

4. Take an outline of one of your earlier speeches. Check it against the 10 specifications of a good outline set forth in this chapter, revise it, and hand it in.

5. Outline the class lecture of one of your instructors. A good class lecture ought to move a little more slowly than a regular public speech, and you should be able to make a full outline as the lecture proceeds.

6. Use the following procedure in planning your next speech:
   a. While still in preliminary form, check the outline against the 10 specifications set forth in this chapter. Revise the outline, but do not make a full revised copy.
   b. Make a Technical Plot, and use it to test each part of the outline. Revise the outline again if necessary.
   c. Make a final copy of both the revised outline and the Technical Plot. Use the outline for rehearsing the final extempore speech.

Chapter 7

MAKING IDEAS CLEAR

anguage is the greatest invention of the human race. Centuries upon centuries went into developing the technique of using language, and some of the best men who ever lived gave their lives to it. Until you gain sufficient mastery of language you don't think efficiently, for ideas become actual only when you can phrase them into words.

You intend to design airplanes, build houses or run a store. Your plans must first be created mentally, in words. You intend to discuss a problem or situation, like current prices or modern poetry. Your ideas are nebulous, until you turn them into words. You think in words, plan in words, talk in words. Yet, as the semanticists properly remind us, these words in themselves have no value. They are merely symbols for things and thoughts. They are like the paper and ink in $10 bills—worth nothing in themselves, but are intangibles that by skillful techniques man has learned to use as indispensable symbols of value.

Words

Later we shall look at the larger units of language but first we shall look at the smallest unit, words.

CONCRETE WORDS

Suppose you say, "He *went* down the street." You tell what happened but not how. Suppose, instead, you find the exact word that tells *how* he went down the street: "He *staggered* down the street," or *strutted, waddled, strode, slunk, sauntered, marched,* or *ambled.* Each carries a brighter picture.

Consider the word *building.* A building where people live is a *residence;* a modest residence is a *cottage;* a pretentious residence is a *mansion.* A building where goods are made is a *factory;* a building where they are stored is a *warehouse;* a building where they are sold is a *store;* a small store is a *shop.* A building where clerical work is done is an *office.* A building where legislators meet is a *capitol.* A building where books are kept is a *library.* A building for dramatic performances is a *theater.* A building for storing motorcars is a *garage.* A building for sheltering horses is a *stable.* A building for keeping dogs is a *kennel.* A building for quartering soldiers is a *barrack.* A building for worship is a *church;* a modest church is a chapel; a bishop's church is a *cathedral;* a pretentious church is a *temple;* a Jewish church is a *synagogue;* a Mohammedan church is a *mosque.*

A word-lazy person could use the general word *building* for each kind of building. The master of language will choose the exact word to communicate the exact thought. The first basic rule of language, then, is this: Choose the concrete word instead of the general.

SIMPLE WORDS

The second basic rule is to choose the shorter simple word instead of the longer complex one. Herbert Spencer noted that simple words learned early in life carry stronger meanings than longer words learned later. A child "says *I have,* not *I possess—I wish,* not *I desire;* he does not *reflect,* he *thinks,* he does not beg for *amusement,* but for *play;* he calls things *nice* or *nasty,* not *pleasant* or *disagreeable.*

S. Stephenson Smith found that the average reading and hearing vocabulary of the man in the street was 9,000 to 10,000 words, plus special trade words and sports slang. (The vocabulary of the average college freshman, he found, was around 14,000 words.) "Any words beyond that range create a 'block' or blackout of meaning." [1]

Most of the effective speakers talking to nation-wide audiences (Franklin D. Roosevelt and Dwight Eisenhower are examples) keep rather well within the 10,000 commonest words. Mine-run speakers don't do so well. They tend to avoid the simple words for long words and phrases. Instead of *have,* they prefer "in possession of." They don't *ask,* but "make application for." They don't *eat,* but "consume." They don't have *homes,* but "places of residence." They are not even *people,* but "individuals." Especially they like those ele-

[1] "Radio Vocabulary," *Quarterly Journal of Speech,* XXVIII (February, 1942), 2.

MADAME PANDIT

As a delegate from India to the United Nations, she was a spokesman of
the East who talked in words that the West could understand.

phant words: "quadripartite," "unilateral," "directive." They can't just say *four-party, one-sided,* and *order.*

The simple word has power than complex words can never have. "He was conveyed to his place of residence in an intoxicated condition." Of such language, Frank H. McClosky said, "Nonsense! If the man was drunk, say he was drunk. 'He was carried home drunk.' "

COLORFUL WORDS

Words not only *mean,* but *suggest.* If you say, "I ate dead hog," it means the same as "I ate roast pork," but suggests something else. Because of word color you may say, "a *gang* of thieves," but not a "gang of angels," for a group of angels is a *band* or *host.* To say, "She is *skinny,*" can never have the same color as, "She is *slender.*"

The color and feeling of a word gives its persuasive power. Rudyard Kipling—whose persuasive words "taught England the meaning of Empire, and the Empire the meaning of England"—said with utter candor in the last interview before his death: "You must bait your hook with gaudy words. I used to search for words in the British Museum. I read mad poets." If misunderstood to mean exhibitionist words or big words, the advice is dangerous; but if you've read Kipling you won't make that mistake.

No rules govern the mastery of word color and feeling, but the English language offers you sharp and flexible tools. Learn to use them to get the effect you want.

Sentences

After words come sentences. For brevity and emphasis we limit the treatment to two techniques in which unskillful speakers most often fail:

USE VERBS, NOT NOUN SUBSTITUTES

The verb is a motor. It propels the sentence. If you want thought power, work the verb hard. Self-made speakers as a rule flinch from using a live verb. They put the heavy load on nouns, then, in place of a live verb, they use the inert "is" or a colorless verb-phrase like "results in." These noun-users can't say "I *think,*" for *think* is a verb packed with power. Instead, they substitute the inert noun, "thought," and the inactive verb, "is." Thereby they get: "It *is* my thought *that.* . . ." Never would noun-users say, "A stitch in time *saves* nine."

That live verb is a fearful thing, so they turn it into a noun and say: "The advantage of timely stitching *is* ninefold." In the same way, "Haste *makes* waste," becomes "Precipitation *entails the negation* of economy."

As a corrolary to using verbs instead of noun substitutes, add the following principles:

1. *Be wary of the form, "It is . . . that. . . ."* Backward syntax, generally poor in writing, is worse in speech. Instead of *"It is* with pleasure *that* I present. . . ." better say, "I *present* with pleasure. . . ."

2. *Prefer active to passive verbs.* Passive verbs are useful, even indispensable. But use them for special effects. For regular duty use active verbs. Someday when you have the time, count the comparative number of active and passive verbs used by Shakespeare and Shaw— or Lincoln and Churchill—and compare the ratio with those in your freshman themes. You might be startled at the higher percentage of active verbs used by masters of language.

STRIP EMPTY WORDS

Two kinds of empty words especially impair communication:

1. *Adjectives and adverbs.* There are two kinds of modifiers. The first is "defining modifiers": *hot* stove, *sharp* curve. They tell something essential. You need them.

The second is "commenting modifiers": *very* necessary, *most* unique. They are excess words. You don't need them. (Ask yourself how a thing can be "very necessary"? Is not "necessary" the ultimate? And what does "unique" mean? How can anything be "most unique"?) Of people who use such language Schopenhauer exclaimed, "I say they are only half-conscious." Note the commenting modifiers used by half-conscious speakers: "very large," "very pleased," "very nice," "most pleasant," "most exceptional." William Allen White, a master of language, said *very* was the most overworked word in the English language, and once told Franklin P. Adams how to get rid of it: "Instead of *very*, write the word *damn*. The proofreader will knock out the *damn*—and there you have a right good sentence." Unfortunately the speaker has no such censor. He must do the job himself.

2. *Compound prepositions and conjunctions.* Fowler in his *Dic-*

tionary of Modern English Usage compiled a list of typical ones to be avoided. Here are a few:

with regard to (about)	with a view to (to)
in the event that (if)	with the result that (so that)
of the nature of (like)	for the purpose of (for)

Supporting Materials

Untutored speakers tend to fill their speeches with general ideas. But general ideas are only abstractions, only assertions about assertions. Listeners, on the other hand, are mere human beings with a limited span of attention. They need to have ideas supported with concrete materials. We have already discussed the elementary phases of this (pages 30-38). We shall now consider it in detail.

SUPPORTING IDEAS BY DEFINITION AND EXPLANATION

"If you would speak with me, define your terms," said Seneca. Napoleon stated the compulsion in different words. To secretaries who relayed his messages he gave three instructions: "(1) Be clear. (2) Be clear! (3) *Be clear!*" To be clear you must define your terms, not merely define them out of a dictionary, but define them as you use them in the speech context. Especially will two types of terms need defining:

1. The first is technical words, or complex words, that listeners won't know. Thousands of such words are in common use by specialized groups but are not known by the general public. Typical of a few appearing in recent student speeches are: *laissez faire* (economics), *median* (statistics), *pragmatism* (psychology), *sonata* (music), *tolerance* (engineering). When you use such words, define them, amplify the definition, illustrate what you mean.

2. Next, are familiar words used frequently and loosely, but which have many meanings to different people. Typical of these are: *democracy, Americanism, socialism*. Typical also are those two-edged words like *justice, right, wrong*. To many people, these words have no real meaning. They have only emotional associations. Unless defined, they become trigger-happy releases for emotions, but without form and void of thought. Speakers must often use them, and ought to use them, but they need to define them if they are to speak with clarity and precision.

Suppose you were discussing "democracy." How would you define it? Is it the same as a "republic"? Is the British "monarchy" also a "democracy"? Note how Henry M. Wriston defines it by: (1) comparison, (2) classification, and (3) testimony:

> We could say of democracy what Lincoln said of liberty: "The world has never had a good definition. . . and the American people, just now, are much in want of one."
>
> . . . . Democracy is not a form of government. It exists within many forms—whenever, in fact, the consensus of mature public opinion governs public action. . . . Democracy must not be confused with ballots or any other procedural device. Instead, it is a spirit which animates political, social, and economic conditions. And the essence of that spirit is profound respect for human dignity. . . .
>
> Respect for individual human dignity is the inner meaning of the most striking phrase of the Declaration of Independence: "We hold these truths to be self-evident,—that all men are created equal." [2]

SUPPORTING IDEAS WITH FACTUAL INFORMATION

"Facts," said Owen D. Young, "are our scarcest raw material." Especially true is this with student speeches. Young people can not often speak with authority. They need the power of facts.

Getting the facts is not easy. You can never get "all the facts," for "all the facts" about the simplest event—like an automobile accident —would fill hundreds of pages: eyewitnesses' reports, the metallurgical engineer's report, the optician's report, the psychiatrist's report. "Getting the facts," then, means getting the pertinent facts.

Selecting the particular facts to be used in a speech becomes a test both of intelligence and character. The selection cannot be "objective," for it is done by human beings who have their own degrees of understanding and their own set of values. Hence there is no such thing as "impartial" facts. What every speaker should seek instead is *fairness*. What is the difference? A responsible speaker is "partial" to that interpretation of facts that seem to fit things as they really are. He is "fair" in "not twisting the facts to support his view, and in not suppressing the facts that support a different view."

The following extracts from a speech of John Foster Dulles, shows effective use of factual information:

> Our first stop was in Egypt. There we had three days in which to get acquainted with General Naguib. . . .
>
> After Egypt we went on to Israel. . . .

[2] *Vital Speeches*, XVI (June 1, 1950), 503.

From Jordan we went to Syria and there we were impressed by General Shisheikly. . . .

In India I met again with Mr. Nehru, one of the great leaders of our time. We had long conversations together in the intimacy of his home. . . .[3]

Figures are an effective form of factual explanation if used wisely and sparingly. You don't want to load a speech with too many figures. Listeners won't remember them, and often won't even try to remember them. But used wisely and sparingly, figures can make clear many an idea otherwise vague. You can say, "Automobile accidents are increasing," but how can you demonstrate this without presenting figures? You can say that "Unemployment is getting better (or worse)," but how can you know—or the audience understand—without figures of comparison with previous years? Senator Albert W. Hawkes wanted to show that "young men had made great achievements." Merely to assert was not enough. He presented figures:

Alexander Graham Bell invented the telephone at 28; George Eastman produced dry plates for photography at 26; George Westinghouse. . . invented the air brake at 22; Henry Ford produced his first motorcar at 29; Thomas Edison. . . invented the incadescent lamp at 32; the Wright brothers were 32 and 36, respectively, at the time of their first air flight; Woolworth established his first store when 24; John D. Rockefeller organized the Standard Oil Co., when 31; John Wanamaker opened his first department store at 31; Lord Byron published his first book of poems at 19; Charles Dickens published his first book of Pickwick Papers at 24. . . .

This is the "march of youth" instead of the "march of time." [4]

Statistics are not the same as ordinary figures. They are groups of facts scientifically collected and classified on the basis of relative number of occurrences as the ground for induction. In short, statistics are a systematic compilation of instances for the inference of general truths. They are widely used in modern life. *But if they are not accurate, or if they are not scientifically classified, they are false and misleading.*

Beware, then, of pseudo statistics:

Tests show that four out of five have it.

Who did the testing? What was the nature of the tests? How representative was the sampling tested?

Last year more Americans were killed by automobiles than were killed in the Korean War. Actually, automobiles are more dangerous than guns.

[5] *Vital Speeches*, XIX (June 15, 1953), 519-520.
[4] *Vital Speeches*, XII (August 1, 1946), 632-633.

But last year white sheep ate more than black sheep, and it proved nothing except there were more of them. Raw figures are not statistics.

In using statistics, therefore: (1) Check their source and determine its reliability. (2) Tell the listeners where you got them. Don't try to cover up their transparent misuse by such phrases as:

"Records prove that. . . ."   [*Whose records?*]
"Figures establish. . . ."   [*What figures?*]
"Statistics show. . . ."   [*Listeners may remember at your expense the adage that there are lies, damned lies, and statistics.*]

SUPPORTING IDEAS WITH ILLUSTRATIONS

"They say I tell a great many stories," said that master speaker, Abraham Lincoln. "I reckon I do, but I have found in the course of a long experience that common people—common people—take them as they run, are more easily influenced and informed by illustrations than in any other way, and as to what the hypercritical few may think, I don't care." [5] As a speaker, Lincoln had two outstanding qualities, both of which every speaker could use with profit: First, he had the ability to analyze a subject so as to present it to others with complete accuracy. Second, *he learned to argue by analogy and to explain by stories.*

"I have seen an audience," said Henry Ward Beecher, "time and again, follow an argument, doubtfully, laboriously, almost suspiciously, and look at one another, as much as to say, 'Is he going right'—until the place is arrived at, where the speaker says, 'It is like —' and then they listen eagerly for what it is like; and when some apt illustration is thrown out before them, there is a sense of relief, as though they had said 'Yes, he is right.' " Beecher also said—and remember this if you want to become a good speaker—that, "Illustrations, while they make it easier for all, are absolutely the only means by which a large part of your audience will be able to understand at all the abstruse processes of reasoning." [6]

There are two kinds of illustrations. The first is *factual.* It tells of an actual event, in this manner:

The greatest center of Polynesian scientific research in the world today is the Bishop Museum in Honolulu. Its brilliant director is Dr. Peter H.

[5] D. K. Dodge, "Abraham Lincoln: The Evolution of his Literary Style," *University of Illinois Studies,* I, No. 1 (May 1900), 35.
[6] (Yale) *Lectures on Preaching* (New York: J. B. Ford and Co., 1872), pp. 157-158.

Buck, son of an Irish father and a Maori mother, a member of the Polynesian race. Dr. Buck fought with distinction with the forces of New Zealand in the World War. His scholarship has won widespread recognition from universities such as Yale where he has taught. He is a man of extraordinary achievements and rare personal charm. He is a man of whom any country could be proud. But he is denied the privileges of naturalization because his mother is of the Polynesian race.[7]

The second kind is *hypothetical*. This is an illustration of what "might have been," or "could be." When Benjamin Franklin wanted to overthrow the popular notion that men should not vote unless they owned property, he used a hypothetical illustration:

> To require property of voters leads us up to this dilemma: I own a jackass, I can vote. The jackass dies, I cannot vote. Therefore, the vote represents not me but the jackass.

SUPPORTING IDEAS WITH SPECIFIC INSTANCES

A Specific Instance is a condensed illustration. It names the person, place, date, or event—but does not develop it by details. For that reason only one or two Specific Instances, without other forms of support, usually is not enough. More likely a battery will be used. Dwight Eisenhower used six:

> This world in arms is not spending money alone. It is spending the sweat of its laborers, the genius of its scientists, the hopes of its children.
>
> The cost of one modern heavy bomber is this: A modern brick school in more than 30 cities.
>
> It is two electric power plants, each serving a town of 60,000 population.
> It is two fine, fully equipped hospitals.
> It is some 50 miles of concrete highway.
>
> We pay for a single fighter plane with a half million bushels of wheat.
> We pay for a single destroyer with new homes that could have housed more than 8,000 people.[8]

Or a speaker may lead with other forms of support, such as an Illustration or Comparison, then reinforce with a battery of Specific Instances. Or he may lead with a battery of Specific Instances and follow with other forms of support, as George Gallup below, who supported his idea with five Specific Instances overtopped by Testimony:

> In a recent survey of college graduates which I undertook. . . only one in ten could name the author of *Tom Jones*; three out of four could not name the author of *Wealth of Nations*; six in ten could not name the author

[7] Joseph R. Farrington, *Vital Speeches*, XI (August 1, 1945), 638.
[8] *Vital Speeches*, XIX (May 1, 1953), 419.

of *Vanity Fair*. One college graduate interviewed frankly admitted that he had not read a book since he left college ten years ago. . . . He "guessed that" Shakespeare wrote *Canterbury Tales*. . . .

You may recall the attention recorded the two political conventions last summer. . . . Even so, only one adult in every four throughout the country could name the two men selected as vice-presidential candidates. . . .

We must begin to understand that the process of learning is a process which must continue throughout life. As Sir Richard Livingstone has said, "Who can suppose that spiritual and intellectual growth ceases and knowledge and wisdom are finally achieved when a university degree is taken, or that the need of knowledge does not grow more urgent with the passing of the years?" [9]

SUPPORTING IDEAS WITH COMPARISON AND CONTRAST

Comparison measures likeness. It connects the known with the unknown, the less familiar with the more familiar. *Contrast* measures opposites. Often we see a thing more clearly when we see its opposite, heightened by contrast. Both make ideas more clear, more vivid, or more interesting.

Sometimes they are brief and pithy, like the traffic expert's description of safety:

The driver is safer when the roads are dry; the roads are safer when the driver is dry.

At other times it is longer, more detailed, and liberal. Observe this detailed and accurate comparison between present Communist aggression and earlier Moslem aggression:

In our short history, we have never had to face any problem as complex as the problem of this Communist assault. The western world did once face a similar problem. The fighting faith of Mahomet overwhelmed the Christian States of the Near East and North Africa and Spain, and the Moslem forces were not stopped until they reached Tours on the Loire not very far from Paris. . . . In the hundred years between Mahomet's death in 632 and the defeat of the Moslems by Charles Martel in 732, country after country fell before that fighting faith until it seemed that it was irresistible.

The Communist attack is no more irresistible than was the Moslem attack. But to meet it successfully, we shall need the same faith and courage that the Christians had at Tours.[10]

SUPPORTING IDEAS WITH TESTIMONY

Often listeners will not take your unsupported word, but will re-

[9] *Vital Speeches*, XIX (May 15, 1953), 474-475.
[10] William C. Bullitt, *Vital Speeches*, XVI (July 1, 1950), 563.

spect the judgment of others. If you assert that the cost-of-living index has gone up or down by 5 points, the statement will carry more weight if you cite the U. S. Department of Commerce as authority. Student speakers especially need the testimony of others.

Testimony is used not only for proof, but also for vividness. Others have stated ideas so vividly that you can often reinforce argument, or make ideas clear, simply by quoting their lucid words. The best thoughts of the greatest minds of all ages have been preserved, and they are yours for the using. In the following example Henry R. Luce, editor of *Time* and no mean authority himself, uses testimony to reinforce thought and to make it vivid:

> We Americans, more than other peoples, need continuously to know who we are, where we are. A good symbol of America is the train of covered-wagons. We are not a fixed people, formed long centuries ago in loyalty to a crown or to a river valley. We create ourselves as a nation as we go along. . . . As Thornton Wilder says so eloquently in a broad context: "Americans are still engaged in inventing what it is to be an American." [11]

Winston Churchill, whose speeches are almost poetry, was especially fond of the testimony of poets:

> I rejoice in Tennyson's celebrated lines:
>
> "Men, my brothers, men; the workers ever reaping
> something new;
> That which they have done but earnest of the things
> that they shall do."

SUPPORTING IDEAS WITH RESTATEMENT AND REPETITION

Study the following example of restatement:

> [1] The answer is very simple. [2] I don't mean easy, but simple. . . . Because it begins at home.
>
> [1] Home is not necessarily a place fixed in geography. [2] It can be a rented room.
>
> [1] But it must be all the rooms or apartments; [2] all the houses on that street [3] and all the streets in that association of streets until they become a whole, an integer of people who have the same aspirations and hopes and problems and duties. . . . [4] Home: not where I live . . . but where *we* live.
>
> WILLIAM FAULKNER, *Before the Final Signature*

You will observe that the speaker presents no proof, and that he cites no Comparisons, Illustrations, or Specific Instances. Instead each separate idea is repeated in different words.

[11] *Vital Speeches*, XIX (April 1, 1953), 371.

This is known as restatement. Its value is obvious. When an idea cannot be understood through one single statement, then restatement gives listeners time to think it over, and digest it slowly as they come to understand its full meaning.

Now study the following example of *repetition.*

> We shall defend our island, whatever the cost may be. *We shall fight* on the beaches. *We shall fight* on the landing grounds. *We shall fight* in the fields and in the streets, and *we shall fight* in the hills. We shall never surrender.
>
> WINSTON CHURCHILL, *After Dunkerque*

Here the speaker repeated the same idea four times in the same words. This is known as repetition. Skillful repetition drives an idea home. It reinforces memory. Skillful repetition also has persuasive force. It helps establish belief. In Shakespeare's version of Marc Antony's speech, Antony starts by saying that Caesar's murderers are "honorable men." But when he repeats "honorable men" nine times, with growing irony, the citizens grasp the intended contrary meaning and rush forth shouting, "We'll burn . . . the traitors' houses."

SUPPORTING IDEAS WITH DESCRIPTION

Description tells how a thing looks, feels, tastes, smells, or how it acts. In words, it recreates places, things, and people for the listener's personal inspection. If you say, "In the Middle West summer winds blow constantly," that is explanatory fact. If you say, "Beginning with moist winds in May and continuing into dry winds in August, the summer winds are constant in the Middle West," you narrate events. But Ernie Pyle *described* those winds so you could feel them blow against your face:

> To me the summer wind in the Midwest is one of the most melancholy things in all life. It comes from far and blows so gently and yet so relentlessly; it rustles the leaves and the branches of the maple trees in a sort of symphony of sadness, and it doesn't pass on and leave them still. It just keeps coming, like the infinite flow of Old Man River. You could—and you do—wear out your lifetime on the dusty plains with that wind of futility blowing in your face. And when you are worn out and gone, the wind—still saying nothing, still so gentle and sad and timeless—is still blowing across the prairies, and will blow in the faces of the little men who follow you forever." [12]

The following are suggestions for effective description:

[12] *Home Country* (New York: William Sloan Associates, Inc., 1947), p. 3.

1. Determine the purpose. Suppose you want to describe a storm, for example. Do you want to tell how it arose and what it did? That is factual. Do you want to demonstrate its power and malevolence? That is imaginative. Do you want to describe a physical thing? Or a mental state? Determine one purpose, and stay by it.

2. Make description brief. Few speakers have the power to hold attention long by description.

3. Follow a systematic order. Describe from right to left, front to back, top to bottom.

SUPPORTING IDEAS WITH NARRATION

Effective speakers know the power of narration. Self-minded introverts do not use it; they are color-blind to human values. Students at first neglect it, for they have not yet discovered its power. Hence, we here pause for narrative identification.

Narrative takes many forms—among which are the illustration, story, historical incident, and anecdote. All have a common element. They do not argue or provoke controversy, but narrate what has happened. They are concrete, interesting, full of action. They can create suspense, or arouse laughter, or depict tragedy.

Good narrative seems so simple and natural that anyone can do it. Unhappily, not so. It, too, has a technique, of which the essentials are these:

1. Tell the events in the order in which they occur.

2. Tell them in the form in which the listener might have seen them.

3. Organize the narration so it goes from somewhere to somewhere else—and sits down when it arrives.

All of these are illustrated in John Mason Brown's radio speech on "A Cartoonist in Words":

Move back in time; a full twenty-five years back. The scene is the New York apartment of T. R. Smith, then the editor of the *Century Magazine*. The hour is a thirsty one, towards twilight, when a long day's work is done. Two men, scarcely unknown, two men who cannot be accused of having a passion for anonymity, have just appeared at Mr. Smith's door. They are H. L. Mencken, and George Jean Nathan. Their job, just then, is to edit the *American Mercury;* their pleasure is to be the Katzenjammer kids of American literature. When Mr. Mencken and Mr. Nathan enter Mr. Smith's apartment, they notice a stranger. He is a tall, skinny, paprika-headed fellow. . . .

The stranger approached them, much as the sea serpent approached the Laocoön group. He coiled one long arm around Mr. Mencken's neck, the other around Mr. Nathan's. Then he started talking. Nathan described it as "yelling at the top of his lungs."

"So you guys are critics, are ya? Well, let me tell you something. I'm the best writer in this here blankety-blank country; and if you, Georgie, and you, Hank, don't know it now, you'll know it blankety-blank soon. Say, I've just finished a book that'll be published in a week or two, and it's the best blankety-blank book of its kind that this blankety-blank country has had and don't you forget it." . . .

The book was *Main Street;* the tall, skinny stranger with the paprika hair was, of course, Sinclair Lewis.[13]

Exercises

1. List the violations of language techniques found in the following passages. Then rewrite and improve them:

    a. It is with very great pleasure that I address you on this most auspicious occasion.

    b. Special emphasis has been placed on miniaturization and ruggedization of new equipment.

    c. It is advisable that one makes an examination of what is ahead before committing oneself to moving forward precipitantly.

    d. It is a very unique book that I have just read, a book in the nature of a biography of Thomas A. Edison. It shows how Edison, even as a boy, was most unusual. It shows how Edison as a man developed into a genius who was most exceptional.

2. Examine one of your old outlines; or, if you have recorded a speech in this course, listen to the playback. Write a brief report on your skill in using each of the five word and sentence techniques discussed in this chapter.

3. In preparing your next speech, check whether you are using language techniques with reasonable skill. In the Technical Plot, left margin of the outline, note where you are making deliberate use of these techniques.

4. Give a 2-minute speech of definition in which you classify, compare, illustrate, and if possible use testimony, in making clear the meaning of technical, complex, or strange word.

5. Give a 2-minute speech of definition on some common word or phrase used loosely by different people, such as *Americanism, freedom, the common man, civil liberty, apple-polisher, straight-laced.*

13 *Talks,* XI (January, 1946), 40.

6. Give a 2-minute speech in which you support an idea with factual information.

7. Give a 2-minute speech supporting an idea with one good illustration.

8. Give a 2-minute speech supporting an idea with half a dozen specific instances.

9. Give a 2-minute speech in which you compare and contrast such ideas as: (1) jazz and bebop, (2) comedy and melodrama, (3) education and training, (4) art and science, (5) town and gown, (6) prose and poetry.

10. Give a 2-minute speech supporting an idea with acceptable testimony from two or more sources.

11. Give a 2-minute speech supporting an idea only with restatement or repetition, or both.

12. Give a 2-minute speech supporting an idea with description, and decide in advance whether you want to make it factual description, imaginative description, etc.

13. Give a 2-minute speech supporting an idea with some form of narration.

Chapter 8

PERSUASION

T here is scarcely a chapter in this book that does not treat persuasion directly or obliquely. Chapter 3 (First Steps in Managing Ideas), Chapter 6 (Organizing the Speech), and Chapter 7 (Making Ideas Clear) treat it directly and almost exclusively. In this chapter, however, we shall discuss the *system* of persuasion by which the procedures previously covered can be used most effectively to influence human attitudes and behavior.

You don't need to be told that people are filled with all sorts of beliefs and attitudes that did not come from reason, or logic, or objective assembling of facts. Now that you are in college, it would be delightful to say that education will change all that—that whereas less educated and less intelligent folk are ruled by prejudice, really intelligent people after they are educated are henceforth ruled by reason; and so when you talk to them all you need is to "know the facts," "assemble the evidence," and "give the reasons." This would be delightful indeed—but total nonsense. Anyone with common sense recognizes the truth of Oliver Wendell Holmes' statement, written after nearly thirty years on the Supreme Court: "As I grow older I realize how limited a part reason has played in the conduct of men. They believe what they want to." This verdict of wisdom is reaffirmed by research. A. T. Poffenberger, psychologist, summarized the results of prolonged experiments on the conditions of belief: "Belief is rarely the result of reasoning. . . . We tend to believe what arouses our desires, our fears, and our emotions."

Persuasion is largely a matter of making others want to believe. In formal public communication it involves four constituent parts:

Hold the Listeners' Attention on the Subject

At the start of a speech you face what H. A. Overstreet calls a "dead-line of interest." To your opening words listeners tend to say,

"*Ho hum!*" and after that, "*So what?*" If you can cross that dead-line of interest, you are a speaker. If you fail to cross it, you are merely one of the unwashed.

So stay out of that bog into which unwary speakers sink—starting with foggy abstractions or dull information. Instead, cross that dead-line of interest in the *first* sentence by kindling a quick flame of interest. How do you do it? In a dozen ways if you know how attention operates. Let us pause to look at it.

Attention is a mysterious activity of the mind. In some ways it is like electricity. We don't even know what it is, but we do know how to produce it and how to control it. Also like certain kinds of electricity, attention does not flow in a steady stream. Some electricity alternates; all attention comes in *spurts,* comes and goes. "How long can you give unbroken attention to a lesson?" a student was asked. "About an hour, I guess," he replied. Well, he cannot; neither could Edison or Einstein. *No human being can give unbroken attention to anything for more than a few seconds at a time. What we call unbroken or sustained, attention is really repeated spurts of attention, each of only a few seconds duration. Unless these repeated spurts of attention are kept on the subject, the mind goes hop-skip-and-jump.*

When you talk, don't assume that listeners will naturally give attention. They won't. People's minds wander while their bodies are seated. They can sit and day-dream. They can give attention only in spots, and go away remembering mere bits of what you say. But you want sustained attention, which means you want to keep listeners' *repeated spurts* of attention on the subject. The ways of holding attention have been established by the centuries, and are now reinforced by experimental psychology. We have already discussed some of them in connection with other fundamentals of speechmaking, especially two:

1. *First is the word techniques for making ideas clear, including the more vivid Forms of Support.* Of all means ever discovered for speakers to hold attention, the most compelling is to give the listener moving pictures in words—by illustrations, specific instances, comparisons, testimony, and narration, etc. (see pages 107-113). These make the idea vivid. They keep it moving. Like a magnet they pull the listeners' repeated spurts of attention back to the subject.

2. *Second is to arrange ideas into a simple, obvious, and meaningful pattern* (see pages 83-87). This prevents listeners from getting

lost. It lets them know where you (and they) have been, where you now are, and to foresee where you are going. In a sense, this is like following a road map. You are more interested in the road because you have the map. You are more interested in the map because you are on the road.

Three additional methods of holding attention will be discussed below.

3. *Suspense.* Suspense is that feeling of uncertainty that quickens our pulses or causes us to lean forward, when a football team is on the one-yard line. It is the pull that leads us to read on in deep interest to the climax of a great story. A speaker can use it in many forms. Wendell Phillips used it in an illustration on Daniel O'Connell's astuteness as a lawyer:

He was once summoned to court out of the hunting-field, when a young friend of his of humble birth was on trial for his life. The evidence gathered around a hat found by the body of the murdered man, which was recognized as the hat of the prisoner. The lawyers tried to break down the evidence, confuse the testimony, and get some relief from the directness of the circumstances; but in vain, until at last they called for O'Connell. He came in, flung his riding-whip and hat on the table, was told the circumstances, and taking up the hat said to the witness, "Whose hat is this?" "Well, Mr. O'Connell, that is Mike's hat."—"How do you know it?" "I will swear to it, sir."—"And did you really find it by the murdered man?" "I did that, sir."—"But you're not ready to swear that?" "I am, indeed, Mr. O'Connell."—"Pat, do you know what hangs on your word? A human soul. And with that dread burden, are you ready to tell this jury that the hat, to your certain knowledge, belongs to the prisoner?" "Y-yes, Mr. O'Connell; yes, I am."

O'Connell takes the hat to the nearest window, and peers into it,— "J-a-m-e-s, James. Now, Pat, did you see that name in the hat?" "I did, Mr. O'Connell."—"You knew it was there?" "Yes, sir; I read it after I picked it up."—"No name in the hat, your Honor." [1]

4. *Activity.* As we go down the street and see a crowd before a store window, it does not take a seer or a psychologist to tell us what is going on. We know there is something *moving* inside the window— a television demonstration, mechanical dummy, or man operating a machine.

In the same way a speech that describes activity, that summons before us living characters and animated scenes, will hold attention.

[1] *Speeches, Lectures, and Letters by Wendell Phillips,* Second Series (Boston: Lee and Shepard, 1891) pages 412-413.

Note how continuous is the activity in the following selection—the walking, talking, and listening.

> For a soldier, the war is not over on the day of armistice. It lingers in the mind and behavior patterns. I would present the testimony of Mr. Justice Oliver Wendell Holmes who fought three years in the Civil War, came out still a young man of twenty-three, entered Harvard Law School and graduated with distinction, became a world authority on *Kent's Commentaries* and on Common Law, and lived to serve exactly fifty years on the Supreme Courts of Massachusetts and the United States. But sixty years after the close of the Civil War, Mr. Holmes said in a moment of complete sobriety, "When the ghosts of dead fifers begin to play in my head, the laws are silent." Once again, across the span of sixty years, he stood at Antietam, or on the Jerusalem Road, and could hear the crack of the skirmishers' muskets, and then the long roll of fire as it came from the main line and the battle was begun. This, after sixty years.

5. *Humor.* One important difference between feeble-minded people and normal people is that the feeble-minded have no sense of humor. Normal people like humor. Especially do they like it in a speech when they are seated together, can listen together, and enjoy it together. They give attention to it. They remember ideas reinforced by humor.

But some humor is cheap, stale, and out of place. In general observe the following:

1. Don't drag in a story by the hind leg with that usual stale beginning, "That reminds me. . . ."

2. Don't label your attempted humor in advance by such openings as, "There was once a Scotsman. . . ." or "Two Irishmen were on a boat. . . ."

3. Avoid wise-cracking, or flippancy in general. In short, don't mistake yourself for a vaudeville actor.

4. If you tell a funny story, use one that is so apt, so much to the point of your speech, that it does not matter whether the audience laughs.

The best humor arises from the clever turn of a phrase, a witty comparison, a comic narration, or the incongruous application of a quotation or well-known maxim. It is woven into the text of the thought. Here is Winston Churchill speaking to the British House of Commons in 1945 shortly after his political party had been defeated

GENERAL MAXWELL D. TAYLOR

The French living in Carentan said that he was the best speaker they had ever heard, because after D-Day he spoke in terms of their self-respect and of the worthwhile service they had rendered.

and the Labor Party had come to power. Observe how he softens opposition by humor:

> They take their politics very seriously in those countries [the Balkans]. A friend of mine, an officer, was in Zagreb, when the results of the late General Election came in. An old lady said to him, "Poor Mr. Churchill! I suppose now he will be shot." My friend was able to reassure her. He said the sentence might be mitigated to one of the various forms of hard labor which are always open to His Majesty's subjects.

Get Listeners to Accept Your Competence and Character

Listeners don't accept or reject ideas merely from the way they are presented. They also accept or reject *because of the person who advocates them.* Before they accept the idea, they must accept *you.* "The reason why anyone refuses his assent to your opinion, . . ." said Emerson, "is in you. He refuses to accept you as the bringer of truth, because . . . you have not given him the authentic sign." There you have it. To be accepted, and believed, *you must give listeners "the authentic sign."*

First are two "signs" to be avoided. Both definitely are not "authentic":

1. Don't say or imply, "Since you don't know much about this subject, I want to tell you about it," or "How many of you ever stopped to realize that . . .?" When you slap listeners, they slap back, silently but viciously: "So you know everything, eh?" or "I realize a lot of things, smart face, that you never will." A persuasive speaker reverses the method: "You remember so-and-so," or "I am sure you realize that. . . ."

2. If you attempt to criticize, include yourself with the audience. Permit no holier-than-thou inference, nothing to suggest that, "I am the judge," and "you are the judged." Say rather "*We* have neglected this problem," or "*We* are caught unawares."

But these are mere preliminaries. The real authentic signs are positive.

1. *Listeners trust the speaker who shows intellectual integrity and sound judgment.* Don't give listeners a chance to call you an exaggerater, or to brand you as being casual with truth. Stay within the bounds of evidence, and far enough within so they know you are not hovering on the border line. Don't pretend to prove more than you

have proved; for what counts is not what you say you have proved, but what listeners think you have proved. All in all, present your case in such a way that those who are doubtful or who disagree will say, "He spoke honestly."

2. *Listeners trust the speaker who seems to know what he is talking about.* They like to know a speaker is qualified to discuss the subject because of his experience or because he has investigated it thoroughly. They like the speaker whose discussion implies, "A part of this I saw," or "For all of this I am personally responsible." Therefore, brace yourself to the duty of testing and processing trustworthy information. Especially, be suspicious of making yourself the mouthpiece of propaganda articles and propaganda books. There are ways of explaining your authority without boasting: "When I was checking some material for this speech, I ran across an unusual book. . . ." Or, "I want to talk about 'How to Study,' because last year my grades told me I did not know much about it, and this year I resolved to inquire into what psychologists knew about it." Or, "I was working last summer on the graveyard shift. . . ."

3. *Listeners trust the speaker who shows moderation, restraint, and good will.* Remember that listeners' beliefs and attitudes are important to them. Usually, they are deep-rooted, and they satisfy deep-felt wants. Therefore, don't attack them outright. Don't even try to make listeners suddenly give them up and take on new ones. Instead, water and cultivate ideas to produce growth and change, just as you would water and cultivate crops to promote growth and harvest. "Make haste slowly," is a proverb to be followed literally.

For the same reason, don't praise or damn indiscriminately—be it Congress, the President, labor, capital, or anything, or anyone. Instead, get your facts, present your case, and let the facts speak. No question is too controversial, if you give listeners light and not heat, and if you do so with moderation, restraint, and good will.

Rest Reason on Listeners' Impelling Wants

Many people assume that a speaker must either "appeal to emotion" or "appeal to reason." A corollary is usually also implied, that "appeal to emotion" is unethical, or at the most is pandering to human weakness, and hence the ideal speaker should "appeal to reason." This notion exists among otherwise highly-educated people, among people who ought to know that it comes from outworn armchair psychology, and that it misses the bases of human behavior. Yet it persists, and we can expect to hear repeated in the future that comment recently made by a well-intended educator: "You should teach students to appeal to reason instead of appealing to emotions."

Students who live in the twentieth century should know that this concept ignores the nature of man. It ignores the motives that down the centuries have led people to struggle for survival and uplift and enlightenment. Man does not live by bread alone, yet "a hungry man is more interested in four sandwiches than he is in four freedoms." Speakers who deal with the diversities of man do not classify their methods into "appeal to emotion" or "appeal to reason."

First, there is no "either-or." Psychologists now know that people do not have compartments, with the "intellect" in one compartment and the "emotions" in another. Reason is not the opposite of emotion any more than wearing good clothes is the opposite of having good sense.

Next, the word "appeal" can be misleading, and often is. If one describes a man walking down the street as "appealing his feet to the sidewalk," you rightly question whether he is using apt language. So with "appeal" in speaking. True, a speaker can use "appeals," but in effective speaking he does not need to, and in fact usually does not. More likely he speaks logically in terms of listeners' wants, hopes, or ideals.

Finally, use of the word "emotion" can be misleading. People have emotions, of course, and they are essential to human life. But effective speakers do not usually deal with them as such. Rather they deal with wants, motives, hopes, ideals, ambitions. Therefore it is better to think in terms of wants, motives, hopes, ideals, and ambitions, than in terms of "emotions."

So let us put aside the notion that we must either "appeal to reason" or "appeal to emotion," and see what actually takes place in operating practice. We know that you don't persuade others merely by "knowing the facts," "assembling the evidence," and by "giving the reasons." These are important. Often they are vital. But they are not enough. The main reason why they are not enough is that man "thinks" and "reasons" under definite limitations. The findings of psychological research on this are well summarized by Daniel Katz: "Analytic thinking occurs not as a prevalent mode of human response but as a limited reaction under conditions of block or need. Men think critically and precisely only under specific conditions of motivation, and then only in reference to the particular pressing problem." [2]

In other words, people think when they get in a jam. In placid times, they drift without using reason, but when they face a real problem and want to know the way out—they use reason, or turn to someone who can use it. Reason, then, is the instrument by which people solve pressing problems and get out of a jam. *The use of reason consequently will always be related to human needs or wants.*

So in persuasion you show people by reason how to solve a problem they need to have solved, how to satisfy a felt want, how to reach a goal, how to move toward an ideal. In other words, in persuasion you rest reason on the listeners' impelling wants.

To do this, of course, you must first know their needs, their hopes, their ambitions, their fears. You must know to "what gods they pray and what kind of fights they love," know what songs they sing, and what sentiments they applaud. There are six human wants that are basic to all relations in life. By no means do these exhaust the list, for civilized man has split and combined and refined his wants into many channels. He has developed institutions—such as governments, churches, schools, and social clubs—to protect and promote them. But these six are deeply rooted in all of us. They are motives on which effective speakers rest their reason and logic and evidence.

SURVIVAL

The most basic want of all is survival. Not mere survival of life alone, but survival on fittest terms. People want to live, and to have food, clothing, and shelter. They want palatable food, and comfortable clothing and shelter. If they are threatened by loss of them, or by lowering of standards, they seek urgently for ways and means to prevent it.

SECURITY

Next to survival is the desire for future security. To be secure from loss of job, to be secure from loss of property or income, to be secure from the uncertainties of tomorrow, even to be secure from having to change our daily habits. It matters not that a courageous few insist that, "There is no security; there is only opportunity." People

---

[2] "Psychological Barriers to Communication," in Wilbur Schramm, *Mass Communication* (Urbana: University of Illinois Press, 1949), p. 277.

want security. Nations want security. They will plan, labor, and pay heavily to gain security.

RECOGNITION

Nobody wants to be that mythical Common Man. We want to be recognized as counting for something, as doing something worthwhile. We want to be the Uncommon Man or Uncommon Woman. This want impels college students to seek athletic honors, or a Phi Beta Kappa key, or to be known for campus activities. It impels people to seek political power, industrial power, social prestige, or to own a bigger house, drive a costlier car, or have a more expensive wedding than others. However high or low our scale of life may be, we want somebody to look up to us.

DIGNITY AND SELF-RESPECT

To do our work well, to live without frustration, we must have a sense of dignity and self-respect. "Let me ask the man . . ." said Lincoln, "what compensation he will accept to go to church some Sunday and sit during the sermon with his wife's bonnet upon his head?" Why is such an act unthinkable? We don't want to be laughed at, or looked down on. It robs us of dignity and self-respect.

WANTING TO BELONG TO SOMETHING WORTHWHILE

We don't want to be left out or by-passed. We want to have extended the glad hand of fellowship, to be taken in and made to feel at home. But merely belonging is not enough. We want to belong to a team that is doing something worthwhile, something that makes us proud of our accomplishment. We want to believe that ours is the best college, best city, best state, best country, or the best group whatever it is. We can be roused to work or serve in order to make it so.

REVERENCE FOR SOMETHING HIGHER THAN OURSELVES

We want to reach out and up to something beyond ourselves. This desire operates on at least three levels. One is *hero worship*. It may be the star on the varsity team, the Sultan of Swat in baseball, a national hero—a Washington or Lincoln, Edison or Henry Ford. We reverence also *tradition*. Among reverenced traditions are Home, Mother, Flag, Democracy, Freedom, Free Enterprise, Science, and the Scientific Method. Finally, there is *reverence for Deity*. "If there were no God," said Voltaire, "it would be necessary to invent one." True. You may

travel across all the face of the earth—from the high plateaus of
Tibet, through the valleys of civilization, into the jungles that are the
last retreat of primitive man—and everywhere you will find worship-
ing men. What they worship may differ. Whether they worship is
never a question.

Speak, then, with respect of things that people reverence or worship.
If you must disagree with tradition, or question the greatness of accepted—do so with extreme tact, and with reverence for other traditions or heroes not in question. Walk softly and speak gently, "for
thou goest among snares and walkest upon the battlements of the
city."

These are the foundations of persuasion. We now come to the ways
and means by which all the procedures of speechmaking previously
studied can be applied to persuasion in a convenient system:

Develop Each Idea According to the Listeners' Attitude

By this we mean that you should consider the attitude of the most
significant part of your listeners toward each part of your speech,
each main head so to speak, then you should develop that part so as
to relate it most effectively to these listeners' wants. For convenience
we shall recognize levels of attitudes:

1. *Is the audience actively favorable?* Then develop the topic by
the IMPRESSIVE OR DYNAMIC METHOD. This consists of telling
people what they already know—old facts, old stories, old ideas.
People like to relive events of the past, to think again of the "good
old days." College graduates return to the campus after many years.
Societies meet to renew old memories. Nations commemorate great
events of their past. A large amount of speaking consists simply of
telling people old things in a new way.

In doing this you do not try to *prove* what listeners already actively
believe. Instead you revive cherished memories and associations. You
vitalize them, give them richer meanings, and surcharge them perhaps
with a drive for action.

The following forms of support will be especially effective:

Illustrations	Description
Specific Instances	Narration
Comparisons	Suspense

2. *Is the audience indifferent?* Then use the MOTIVATIVE METHOD to show why the subject is important. Is it a problem dimly seen that will soon become acute? Is it a neglected problem about to take listeners unawares? Is it a once-settled problem that now returns to life? Is it a perennial and unpleasant problem that we want to forget and Let George Do It?

Suggested modes of development are these:

Motivate it by showing the involved wants, needs, hopes, and ideals. Possible forms of support for this are:

Facts and Figures	Explanation
Testimony	Restatement

Vitalize it by making the ideas vivid. For this the following are especially effective:

Illustrations	Description
Specific Instances	Narration
Comparisons	Suspense

3. *Is the audience doubtful or uninformed?* Then develop the topic by the INSTRUCTIVE METHOD. If listeners are uninformed, or doubtful, you do not develop the topic in the same way as if they knew a great deal about it and already believed it actively. You develop the topic now by presenting information—accurate information, clear information, interesting information. Matthew Arnold said that *we do not change our minds as the result of logic and refutation; but as we learn more, the ground gently shifts beneath us, and we no longer look at things as we formerly did.*

The speechmaker has an important part in this process. There is abundant information available to people today, but much of it is not in usable form. It is false information, or propaganda manufactured to mislead, or simply raw facts that are unprocessed and unrelated to people's needs. The speaker's task is to process them for human consumption.

In presenting such information, a speaker will not dogmatically state his conclusions at the beginning, as if to say: "I am going to prove that thus-and-so are the facts of this case, and that all who say otherwise are impostors." A good speaker does not think that way, nor talk that way. Rather he asks listeners to consider the problem with him: "What are the facts on this question?" or "What caused this problem to become acute?" Having focussed interest, he then proceeds to make clear the answer.

Especially useful are the following methods of making ideas clear:

Defining your terms	Facts and Figures
Explanation	Illustrations
Restatement and Repetition	Specific Instances
Testimony	Comparisons

4. *Is the audience opposed?* Then develop the topic by CONCIL-IATION PLUS IMPELLING ARGUMENT. "Why try such a thing?" someone will say. "Who ever heard of anyone changing his mind because of a speech?" Well, people *do* change their minds in this changing world. The doubtful can be convinced that education is a paying investment, that here is the opportunity of a lifetime, that salvation is free, and that the world comes to an end next Monday night. Changes of opinion do not come from reading a single book or listening to a single speech, but rather from continuous watering and cultivating of ideas.

People who understand humanity have always sold goods and won votes, lifted men's faces toward new ideals, and sent them forth for the Holy Grail. But they have not done it without understanding and harnessing the submerged drives that impel people to action. The steps in this process are relatively simple to set down in print, but exceedingly difficult to follow in practice. Basically there are four:

a. *Don't provoke argument.* An opposed listener is like a cocked gun. It takes only one small pull of the trigger to discharge the full blast. Refrain, therefore, from name-calling and using hate-provoking words like "*Radical* labor leaders," "*Selfish* business interests." Students find it hard to refrain from name-calling. They hold in until the pressure mounts, then relieve it by one hefty name-calling term which they hope won't do any harm. But one is enough. Like Mercutio's wound, it may not be as wide as a church door, or as deep as a well, but it will do the business in the end. Face it frankly. Name-calling is an index of character. People without restraint of character will obviously name-call. Before favorable audiences it is effective. Before opposed audiences it is self-inflicted injury.

b. *Seek first to get a Yes-Response.* Says one speaker "Politics on this campus are rotten, and every campus office holder got there by secret bargaining." Listeners who voted for the winning candidates, in their own mind, retort "No! That's false!" This "No" is far more than merely uttering a silent word. It sets the whole pride of the listener's personality against the speaker. No matter if later the listener feels that his "No" was ill-advised. To save face he must stand by it. But another speaker says, "How many of us are proud of this institution? How many of us wish we had gone somewhere else?" Everybody is *with* the speaker as he continues: "I want to talk about campus politics. We must have campus politics, of course, for we can't have officers without candidates, nor candidates without supporting groups." To all this the listeners say, "Yes," as the speaker continues: "Now what about the last campus election? A faculty-student committee has investigated it, and gives the following summary. . . ." So far, not a listener has had much chance to say "No." The first speech committed suicide in the opening sentence. The second will go far.

c. *But beware of being ingratiating.* Listeners will not be fooled, and they will not be mocked. They will see through insincerity as through cellophane. They will see both faces of a two-faced speaker. Call two-facedness what you will: apple-polishing, soft-soaping, laying-it-on, or other names less printable that students all know—it all comes to the same end. To seek common ground for a Yes-Response is a way of honestly trying to settle differences by talk, a way of learning to live with other people. To talk out of the other side of your mouth is quite something else. It does not require intelligence to distinguish between them, though it may require character to separate them in practice.

d. *Follow up by developing the subject so that hearers either* (*1*) *forget their objections, or* (*2*) *have them removed by logical processes.* It is a curious commentary on human nature, but true one, that some people can be persuaded simply by causing them to *forget* their objections. Thus vivid description, moving illustration, sustained attention of any sort, may serve to persuade. But frankly this is not the best method. The other and more effective method is to follow up by impelling argument (not to be confused with "provoking an argument"). The method of impelling argument is not so much argument as it is carefully organized *information*, related to listeners wants, hopes, aspirations, or ideals.

Exercises

1. From *Vital Speeches* or other sources study the introduction to three speeches. Imagine yourself sitting in each audience, and decide whether the speech would get your attention at the beginning if effectively spoken. Don't be discouraged if most, or all, of these introductions seem to fail. Remember that most speeches today (though conspicuously not all) are given by people who may be experts on their subjects, but who have never learned the techniques of speaking.

2. Make an outline of one of the persuasive speeches printed in the back of this book. Make also a Technical Plot (see pages 93-98 for an explanation of Technical Plots) in which you set down in details the steps and procedures in persuasion that were used by the speaker.

3. Go to hear a speaker, and while he is speaking make a key-word outline of his address. Later, but while the speech is still fresh in mind, expand this into a full-content outline. In the Technical Plot set down the

steps and procedures in persuasion that were used. Also note any essential ones that were missing.

4. Make a full-content outline including the Technical Plot for one or more of the speeches given in class. After studying the speaker's method, as revealed by this outline, write a brief critique of the speech that *will be helpful to the speaker in future talks.*

5. Prepare and deliver a speech to persuade. As you know (see pages 78-81) there are two levels of persuasion: (1) to Stimulate, and (2) to Convince. You may attempt either one, depending on the listeners' attitude to your proposition, but you should know which you are attempting. The following suggestions may be helpful:

   a. Choose a subject about which you are concerned, and on which you have thought for a long time.

   b. Reinforce your own ideas and experiences with material gathered from the library. Talk with others. Be alert to materials that always come to a speaker who is on the lookout.

   c. Follow the steps and procedures of persuasion set forth in this chapter.

   d. Don't try to be an authority on government, politics, or world affairs. If you need it, get authority, and tell when and where authority testified.

   e. Don't use this speech as an excuse for airing thinly-veiled prejudices. Don't damn or praise indiscriminately Russia, China, Congress, the President, Labor, Management, or anything or anyone.

   f. Instead, if you discuss a controversial issue, get your facts (and be sure they *are* facts), assemble your ideas, rest them on impelling wants, and present them to listeners. Hit as hard as you want with the facts, but do not name-call or sing a hymn of hate. No question is too hot to handle, but mud throwing does not solve problems.

   g. Don't pretend to have proved more than you really have proved. In short, don't give listeners a chance to call you a falsifier or exaggerator. So present your case that even those who disagree will say willingly, "He was honest and fair."

Chapter **9**

HANDLING DEMONSTRATION
EQUIPMENT AND VISUAL AIDS

C harts, diagrams, maps, models, and pictures are important aids in explaining difficult or technical subjects. A statistical
curve or plan of battle is more easily demonstrated from a map or
blackboard than from word-of-mouth description. An airplane design
or the anatomy of a vertebrate is better understood from a drawing,
a model, or a specimen. With films and slides you can bring distant
scenes to the audience.

But the use of visual aids is not foolproof. After listening to the
fumblers for twenty-five years, J. R. Van Pelt summarized their abuse
of visual aids "on a thousand platforms" as follows:

We have seen overcrowded slides projected by machines that could not
be focussed. We have watched while speakers in a large room tried to use
maps or charts that could not be read beyond arm's length. We have listened
in vain as able scholars talked confidentially to a blackboard while writing
illegible symbols with invisible chalk. We have fidgeted, mentally if not
physically, as the remarks of a renowned scientist came to a dead stop while
he readjusted some ill-arranged piece of apparatus or hunted for a scientific
specimen to illustrate his point. The habit of using bad visual aids is rampant
among those who "speak to inform." It is an occupational disease of university professors. Severe epidemics break out at every scientific, engineering,
and medical convention.[1]

In short, the sad average of self-made speakers fails to meet the
minimum standard. Let us, then, examine the techniques of using
visual aids.

[1] "Lantern Slides and Such," *Quarterly Journal of Speech*, XXXVI (February,
1950), 45.

Using Charts, Maps, and Diagrams

The rules are simple enough, but the mistakes are many and costly:

1. *Make the charts large enough to be seen.* If the design on a chart is not large enough to be seen, it will be only an annoyance. Do not guess at the proper size, or try to decide about it while standing near by. Draw an experimental chart or diagram beforehand, and go to the back of the room to see whether its outlines can be easily seen in detail. If in doubt, make it larger.

Next, make the lines of the chart or diagram heavy and broad. A light, thin line which is perfectly visible to the speaker up close to it may be barely visible or wholly invisible from the back of the room. Even the writing on a blackboard ought to be carefully checked for size and heaviness of line. Very often blackboard writing is so small and light that persons at a distance cannot read it easily, if at all.

In military training certain sizes of maps and charts are standardized, having been found to be the most effective size. In drawing maps to explain large military operations, for example, before an audience of one hundred or less, a scale of 3 inches to the mile is commonly used. This is large enough to show terrain features, cities, and other necessary items, yet small enough to show a large area of operations on one map or blackboard. Close-ups of military operations, however, are often mapped 6 inches to the mile.

The use of different colors on maps and diagrams may also help to make distinctions clear. For example, a blackboard diagram of the human anatomy may show bones in white, nerves in yellow, cartilages in green, and muscles in red.

2. *Do not crowd too many details into one chart.* Too many details lead to confusion. They distract attention and provoke curiosity. Therefore, cut details and stick to bare essentials. In most charts cut the title, since that is covered in spoken context. Remember that an audience can read only 10 to 20 words without losing the speaker's thread of thought.

If there are several explanations to be made, or a series of steps in a process to be explained, do not try to put them all on one diagram. Instead, use a series of diagrams, each as simple as possible, and put only *one* central idea on each. When you put several points on one chart, the audience races ahead and speculates about the others

**THE FOUNDATIONS OF OUR CIVIL LIBERTIES
AND SOME OF THE DANGERS THAT MENACE THEM**

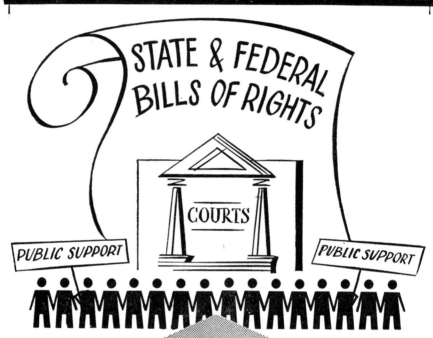

STATE & FEDERAL BILLS OF RIGHTS

COURTS

PUBLIC SUPPORT   PUBLIC SUPPORT

GOVERNMENT INFRINGEMENTS	PRIVATE ATTACKS
UNJUST DENIAL OF MAILING PRIVILEGES TO NEWSPAPERS	RACE ANTAGONISM
EXCESSIVE WARTIME RESTRICTIONS	RELIGIOUS INTOLERANCE
	ABUSE OF MINORITIES
WITCH-HUNTING COMMITTEES	POPULAR HYSTERIA
POLICE BRUTALITY	LABOR EXCESSES

PICTOGRAPH

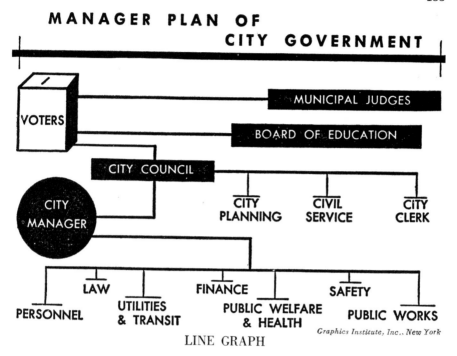

LINE GRAPH

Graphics Institute, Inc., New York

while you are talking about the first one. Therefore, use a series, each as simple as possible.

In general, *graphs* are better than tables when the data permit; that is, when they show systematic trends, patterns, or comparisons. Graphic data are especially applicable where the information can be put in picture form, like the structure of the atom, the shape of a bacillus, or a column comparison of the cost of living today *vs.* ten years ago. Among the most useful kinds of graphs are:

Curves or line graphs on a background of coordinates. For example a curve could show the rise and fall of the value of the dollar since 1900, and the coordinates would indicate each ten-year period.

Bar graphs that emphasize how two sets of facts compare with each other. For example, one bar could represent industrial production ten years ago, and a second bar represent industrial production today.

Pictographs using a row of pictorial symbols in which each represents a different quantity. For example, a large man might represent the number of students in elementary school, a smaller man represent the number in high school, and a still-smaller man represent the number in college.

3. *Talk to the audience instead of to the chart.* The young speaker finds a chart or a diagram to be a welcome refuge from the eyes of

his listeners. He tends to turn away from them and to fix his gaze on the blackboard. Soon he is talking to the blackboard instead of to the audience. Of course, he feels silly talking to a blackboard in a strong and positive tone, and so he begins to mumble.

Do not look at the blackboard except when pointing to something specific on it. Even then, a glance is enough to give you the location, and you can turn again to the audience. *Learn the art of keeping a pointer properly placed on the blackboard while you are looking at the audience.*

4. *Do not stand between the audience and the chart.* The fault opposite to ignoring the audience while talking to the blackboard is that of ignoring the blackboard while talking to the audience. Remember that your chart or diagram has been put on the board because the audience needs to see it. Stand out of the way so they can see it completely. If the audience is seated close to you, this usually means that you must stand at least *three or four feet* to one side. In such situations it is best to use a pointer; this enables you to stand far enough away to keep out of the audience's line of vision.

5. *Do not let an unused chart distract attention.* If possible, charts ought to be kept out of sight until needed, and removed from sight when they are done with. The moment a chart appears, people will look at it and try to figure out what it means; so, if you put up a chart before you want to use it, *the audience will look at it instead of observing and listening to you.* Cover it up, therefore, or keep it out of sight until you are ready for it. Re-cover it, remove it, or erase it when you have finished with it.

Using Pictures and Slides

The use of pictures and slides presents certain additional problems:

1. *Use a screen large enough for the image to be easily seen.* It is doubtful whether the standard small screen, the 39x48-inch size, ought to be used where anyone in the audience is seated more than 35 feet away. At least, many people without perfect eyesight even when they are wearing glasses do not easily see so small an image beyond that distance. Use a larger screen so that people, even those without perfect eyesight, can easily see.

2. *Have the room adequately dark.* For graphs and the like complete darkness is not at all necessary, and is even undesirable. Better simply turn out the lights closest to the screen and get a satisfactory balance between room lighting and screen lighting. This has the advantage of the audience being able to see the speaker, which is always a distinct advantage.

The ideal room for pictures, of course, is completely dark, but pictures must often be shown in rooms that are not ideal, rooms where a certain amount of daylight filters in. How much daylight can be safely allowed depends on the quality of screen and the amount of light the projector can throw. No rule can be given. Therefore, when in doubt *test* the room ahead of time. Then if necessary it can be darkened by draperies, curtains, shades, tar paper—anything at hand, even blankets and stuffing paper into cracks—until the screen image is obviously bright enough from all parts of the room.

Color pictures, be it noted, require a very much darker room and a brighter screen light than black-and-white, because in color pictures the brilliancy of hue depends on the darkness of the room. If even a small amount of outside light filters into the room, it will change the color hues. The effect is literally as though one had mixed paint to exactly the right tint for an especially attractive interior decoration, then, when the color was exactly what was wanted, one dumped into it a bucket of white paint. White light (sunlight) that filters into a room where color pictures are being shown has the same effect as white paint being poured into colored paint. The original color is faded out and a pale, sickly cast remains.

3. *Use a projector that throws plenty of light.* Frankly, many projectors, made to sell inexpensively, simply do not throw enough light to show a good image. The light bulb on the inside may be strong enough (this is often stressed in selling the machine); but it is the speed of lens that determines how much of this light is thrown on the screen. In projectors having a low-speed lens not enough of the light in the bulb is thrown on the screen. Therefore, test your projector ahead of time and learn whether it really throws enough light for the size of your audience.

4. *Do not seat members of the audience directly behind the projector.* No matter how well housed a projector may be, a certain amount of light escapes. This escaping light strikes the pupil of the eye of any person behind the projector, *causes the pupil to contract,*

and so makes it difficult for the person to see the image on the screen. If your projector is set up in the room itself, and not housed in a booth, either place it behind the entire audience (this is by far the best method), or move your audience out of the V zone of light behind the projector. (*See diagram.*)

5. *Pay especial attention to making yourself heard and understood.* For three reasons speakers who are using moving pictures and slides tend not to make themselves adequately heard.

First, they are speaking in the dark where the audience cannot see them. The speaker's nod of the head, turn of the body, or indication of an idea with the hand are lost. The audience now must depend on the speaker's voice alone. That speaker who does not truly project his tones, who compels the audience to a partial lip reading, is now wholly ineffective.

S = *Screen,* P = *Projector,* V = *Zone in which audience should not be seated.*

Second, if the speaker operates his own machine (and there are obvious advantages in the speaker's doing so), he must speak from the rear of the audience or perhaps from the rear of center. The picture is in front of the audience, but the speaker's voice comes from behind. This creates a mental interference, perhaps even a physical interference, *unless the speaker uses enough energy to build up room resonance so that the direction of voice is secondary to its easy audibility.*

Third, if moving pictures are being used, the projector makes a continuous noise. This noise, although not loud, is *at a pitch that masks the intelligibility of the speaker's words.* Therefore, unless the speaker realizes this and uses adequate energy of utterance to override the projector noise, he may quite literally be *heard* but not *understood.*

Exercises

1. Use charts or diagrams to explain some technical subject. Possible examples would be:

   an airplane design (or a comparison of two airplane designs)

   the automatic telephone

   transmission of photographs by radio

   how to navigate a ship or airplane

   how an adding machine works

   how synthetic rubber is made

   weather movements

2. Use a blackboard drawing to illustrate a subject such as the following:

   a famous battle such as Yorktown, Gettysburg, D-Day in Normandy, *Monitor* vs. *Merrimac*, the Naval Air Battle at Saipan, the Inchon Landing

   the geographical importance of: the Suez Canal, oil in the Near East, etc.

   the crayfish

   the human eye

3. Use a specimen or model for demonstrating a subject like the following:

   how an airplane flies

   wood

   the human larynx

   book bindings

   advertising methods

CARRYING ON GROUP DISCUSSION

The term "discussion" does not include the aimless talk that goes on in unorganized groups. Such talk may be interesting. It may be profitable. But it is not "discussion" in the special historical sense of this term. True "discussion" occurs when people meet to consider a common problem. It occurs when they exchange information and ideas, then critically evaluate the information and ideas. Discussion, in short, is a way of thinking together critically through purposeful conversation.

Types of Discussion

Discussion is found in many places and at many levels: in clubs, in churches, in dormitories, in the classroom, in committees and conferences, before public audiences, over radio and television. Often it is not skillfully directed and makes little progress, yet some of the rudiments are there. At other times it is done formally and skillfully. Sometimes the problems talked over are of little concern to anyone except those present. At other times the issues concern large groups of people, even the nation or the world. But we shall consider here only those forms of discussion that are most useful to small groups:

INFORMAL GROUP DISCUSSION

Here a group of ten or twenty persons sit around a circle, or some form of close group, and talk about a subject of mutual interest. There is no audience and there are no formal speeches. No one is a special authority on the topic and no one has made any special preparation. The group simply converses under the guidance of a chairman. The leading purpose is to share information, in the hope that perhaps ideas will evolve or coalesce.

This type of discussion is often difficult to keep within bounds and to keep moving profitably through the various steps of the problem. Members may spend too much time on some early interesting aspect, and so never get very far into the problem. Or they may turn up a new subject entirely, drop the old one and follow the new one. Often the discussion is barren simply because the members do not know enough about the topic; for the collective ignorance of a group does not add to the individual knowledge of any member, nor do ideas coalesce in a vacuum.

With all of its shortcomings, however, the rudiments of discussion are there. If the members understand the problem-solving nature of discussion and are grounded in the steps of logical thinking, informal group discussion can be profitable as well as interesting. Even when it makes no attempt to reach a decision or solve a specific problem, the pooling of thought can be profitable, and the cultivation of ideas can aid growth.

COOPERATIVE INVESTIGATION

This is a splendid method for training in discussion. It involves eight steps:

1. The discussion group meets in advance and elects a leader. The subject is then divided into a number of subtopics, and each member undertakes to investigate at least one of these subtopics.

2. The leader may hold one or more meetings, so that members can know what others have done, and can work out final plans.

3. When the discussion meeting is held, the leader *analyzes and defines* the problem.

4. Each investigator then presents his information in a brief report. *The report contains no argument*, but only information set forth in concise and orderly form.

5. When these reports have all been made, the leader calls for any other pertinent information that members may have.

6. The leader may, if he desires, succinctly summarize the information thus pooled. Then he opens the meeting to a discussion of what ought to be done in the light of the facts thus presented. Possible solutions are not debated, but are talked over with one specific goal in mind: *How can we settle this problem so that it is settled right, and will stay settled?* Disadvantages of the possible solutions are carefully probed, and each possible way for overcoming them is considered. If one particular item of discussion excites the members' emotions, a wise leader will set it aside—put it in the refrigerator, so to speak, to cool. (In Quaker meetings and on certain corporation boards, some topics remain for years in refrigeration before they

can be discussed without tension. Such groups believe that unless emotions are at a minimum, and the consideration of facts are at a maximum, they cannot settle a problem so it will stay settled.)

7. Finally, if the nature of the problem permits, the ways and means are considered for putting into operation the solution agreed on.

8. At the end the leader once more may give a brief summary of the adopted procedure.

This is approximately the method used (they simplify it but do not change it basically) by such groups as city councils, boards of education, church boards, adult education groups, women's clubs, Boy and Girl Scouts, 4-H Clubs, etc.

THE PANEL FORUM

The "panel" portion of the Panel Forum is composed of a chairman and a small group, usually from two to six, who discuss a problem before an audience. They sit at a table where the audience can see them easily.

Of course, the chairman, and the panel members have prepared carefully for the discussion. They follow much the same procedure as that set forth above for the Cooperative Investigation, but one new feature is added. Panel members must talk loud enough for persons in the audience to hear. There are no formal speeches. No one talks for more than a minute or two at a time, and, on the average, members talk much less than that. The members remain seated. Sometimes they talk to one another, sometimes they address the chairman, and at other times they talk directly to the audience—but always they will talk so that people in the audience can hear them easily.

When the panel has explored the problem, the chairman gives a brief summary of what has been said and then turns the meeting into a forum (hence the name Panel Forum) by opening the discussion to members of the audience. Approximately half the available time should be reserved for audience participation.

A panel discussion is essentially conversational, and hence is better adapted to small audiences than to large ones. For a large audience the symposium discussion, explained below, is better.

THE SYMPOSIUM FORUM

This comes closer to formal public speaking than any of the types previously discussed, and hence is especially adapted to large audiences. The "symposium" part consists of a chairman and several

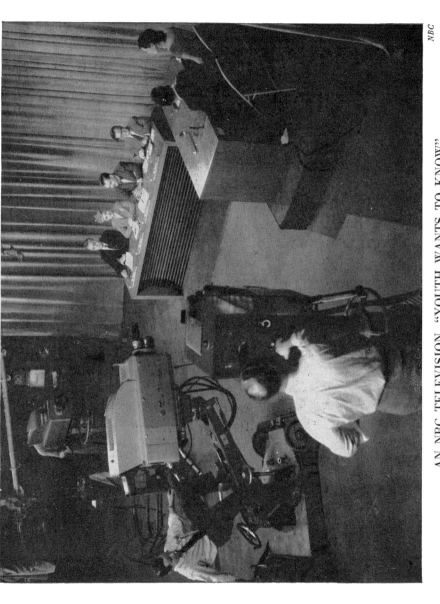

AN NBC TELEVISION, "YOUTH WANTS TO KNOW"

The three cameras shift back and forth from the interviewers (right) to the panel members (left).

speakers, usually two, three, or four. The chairman formally presents each speaker and tells his qualifications as an authority. The speakers stand up and address the audience formally. They do not engage in debate, and their speeches are not simply three or four unrelated addresses on the same topic. Instead, they are attempts to present "thought in process." Each tries to add information and raise pertinent questions. Each reflects a representative approach to the problem.

Then the chairman turns the meeting into a forum by inviting the audience to participate in a question period. These questions get additional information from the speakers, fill in the gaps, weaken or strengthen the arguments already presented. They may be submitted to the chairman in writing, or the questioner may stand and ask his question directly.

THE COMMITTEE MEETING OR CONFERENCE

These discussions ordinarily are not held in public. When an organization cannot discuss all of the business that comes before it, some of the problems are referred to committees which are composed of members having special qualifications. A chairman is designated by the organization, or elected by committee members. The committee meets and discusses the problem, prepares a formal report, and presents it to the organization. Such a committee usually follows the Cooperative Investigation method discussed above.

Conferences are sometimes held publicly. Committee hearings, like those of Congress, are sometimes conducted publicly. The speakers may appear voluntarily or may be subpoenaed. They face the chairman and present a prepared statement, then the committee members follow by prolonged and searching questions. If open to the public, the audience does not participate. It simply sits and listens.

Stating the Discussion Question

Not all questions can be discussed. We do not discuss questions that call for measurable facts, such as who ran the fastest mile or who is mayor of Denver; we simply investigate and find out. Nor do we discuss nonsense questions such as that poser of the Middle Ages, "How many angels can dance on the point of a pin?" If you must know the answer to that one, you can find it by producing the pin and angels, and counting them. Discussion will not help.

We discuss problems that concern our welfare. By discussing them we attempt to find the causes of our difficulties and to arrive at suitable solutions. When a question so concerns us, the first step is to state it precisely. Two suggestions on phrasing questions may be helpful:

1. State the question so it is limited to one specific problem. If you try to discuss such a multiple question as, "Should the powers of the United States Federal Government be reduced and those of the United Nations be increased?" you will find that it involves at least four specific and separate questions, as follows:

1. Should the powers of the United Nations be increased?
2. Should the powers of the U. S. Federal Government be decreased?
3. If they are decreased, should all powers taken from it be transferred to the United Nations?
4. Or, if they are decreased, should some of the powers be transferred to the forty-eight states?

You cannot discuss four intermixed questions at one time, or two. Limit your question to *one* specific problem.

2. State the question so the answers will not be "yes" on one side and "no" on the other. If, for example, you state the question as, "Should the United States maintain a policy of reciprocal trade agreements with foreign nations?" The discussion will turn into a downright debate, with one side arguing "yes" and the other arguing "no." Each side will try to *prove* its case, and neither will be primarily concerned with constructive ideas on foreign trade.

On the other hand, if you state the question as, "How can the United States best develop its foreign trade?" neither side can argue "yes" or "no." In fact, *there will not be any sides,* and the discussion will more likely evoke constructive ideas about improving foreign trade, including the effect of reciprocal trade agreements.

Qualities of Good Group Discussion

To the inexperienced, good discussion may sound like good ordinary conversation, lively and informal, and, of course, interesting. But, underneath, it is fundamentally different. It is *planned* conversation. It starts at a given point and goes through the definite steps of defining and exploring and solving a problem. *It requires a knowledge of the processes of thinking.*

This process involves six steps:

1. What is the *nature* of the problem confronting the group?
2. What *caused* the problem?
3. What are the *several possible solutions?*
4. What are the *advantages and disadvantages* of each?
5. What, finally, seems to be the *one best solution?*
6. How may this solution be *put into operation?*

Of course, intelligent discussion does not plod automatically through each of these Six Steps. Naturally, people who are talking over a problem take stock of the situation, consider where they stand, and how far they may safely or wisely go. Perhaps they already know the nature of the problem (Step 1). Perhaps they even know what caused it (Step 2). The discussion would then pass over these aspects of the question and go at once to the possible solutions (Steps 3). At another time there might be only one possible solution; consequently, the focus of discussion would be on how to work this solution into tangible form and put it into effective operation (Step 6).

Still again, the problem may be so complex that it cannot be solved in the near future, and has not yet developed far enough to determine which one solution is best. At the moment, the only thing to be done is to consider the nature of the problem and its causes, and to develop the several possible solutions which might be adopted—then wait for time to reveal which of them is best (Steps 1, 2, and 3).

How to Participate Effectively

ACQUIRE AND ORGANIZE INFORMATION ON THE SUBJECT

People who know little or nothing about a subject cannot discuss it intelligently or with profit, nor can they form trustworthy opinions on it. They can only pool their ignorance. Before intelligent discussion is possible, the participants must have information. Before they can form judgments, they must have facts. When you are assigned to a discussion, then, your first task is to prepare.

First, think over what you know about the problem, and jot down the main points in a concisely organized outline.

Second, investigate the subject systematically and thoroughly. The *Reader's Guide* in your library will contain a list of magazine articles written on the subject. New issues of this publication appear semi-monthly, and hence it is kept continuously up to date. Generally it is unwise not to consult the *Reader's Guide* and to find out what others have recently written on the subject. Other sources are valuable also: the library card catalogue of books, encyclopedias, yearbooks, government publications, and material published by various private organizations.

Third, read systematically and take notes on what you read. By the aid of notes you can keep information at hand for constant reference. You can also be sure of exact facts, dates, quotations, or opinions.

Fourth, organize your information once more into a concise outline. You may write the outline on paper or arrange it on cards. If you put it on paper, it is quickly visible to the eye. If you put it on cards, the outline can be more complete and detailed than it ordinarily would be if it were written on paper.

TAKE PART IN A COOPERATIVE SPIRIT

Please remember that a discussion is not a contest. It is not a debate. You don't try to score a point, to prove that your "side" is right or that the other "side" is wrong. There really are no "sides" in a discussion. There are only different viewpoints among people who are concerned for the common good of all. You don't try to prove yourself clever or witty, or to stand out as a big shot. You are one of a group that is *thinking together*, and anything that disrupts the process of thinking together is out of place. When you take part, put aside intense individualism and the desire to excel, to dominate the group, or to insist that others accept your ideas.

Learn, instead, to think and feel and talk in terms of group welfare, and to cooperate with others in thinking on the problem. For example, don't sit with an impatient air of one who is waiting to interrupt and get the floor. *Learn to listen,* and to digest what you hear. Ask questions when you need further information, but don't talk too glibly or let go with half-formed ideas. Don't jump on an idea just because it is not yours. Rather consider what good there is in it, and whether it has drawbacks and weaknesses. If you think the idea is good, say so when it comes your turn to talk. If you think there are drawbacks and weaknesses, call attention to them, but always in the spirit of cooperation, of trying to make the idea better rather than to kill it.

Above all, get rid of the idea that your opinions are sacred merely because they are yours. If you present an opinion, and weaknesses appear after others have worked it over, don't let pride get the better of you. Listen to what the others say, and work with them in improving the idea. Ask questions and invite opinions on how to do it. You have met to work out a problem. As nearly as is humanly possible, rise above biases and emotional tensions. Commit yourself to an open-minded search for facts, to a mutual sharing of ideas, to proper sympathy for the attitudes of others, and to thinking *with* the group. Remember that "he who has learned to disagree without being disagreeable has discovered the most valuable secret of a diplomat." Especially carry in mind what the Quakers long ago set down in their Book of Discipline: Experience has demonstrated "that the final decision of a group is usually superior to that of the individual." This is why groups pool their knowledge and experience.

BE SENSITIVE TO TECHNIQUES THAT MAKE THE DISCUSSION PROFITABLE TO LISTENERS

A constant hazard of discussion is that it becomes profitless talk. It not only becomes profitless by ignoring the processes of thinking and by straying from the point at issue. It also become profitless by ignoring the listener. Here are a few obvious precautions that participants should keep especially in mind:

First, be sure that all listeners can easily hear, even when you are overtly talking to other discussion members. This seems too obvious to put in print, yet it is the most common cause of failure, the failure to include the entire audience in the range of audible speech. The discussion members simply do not reach and share their ideas with all the listeners.

Second, remember that when you enumerate points, "1, 2, 3," they are far more listenable than when you make three points without enumeration.

Third, address other participants directly, rather than toss an idea into thin air or pick up another speaker's point without referring to him. For the listener this gives the discussion a personal touch, and gives it movement.

Fourth, always restate a question that is not clearly worded or audibly spoken, whether the question comes from another member or from the floor. It irritates listeners for a speaker to answer a question mumbled by someone down front. The answer is pointless, for listeners don't know the question.

Fifth, keep the ball rolling. Remember that sooner or later it will be tossed to you when you don't expect it, so be ready always to handle it. Keep noting mentally what you would say. If necessary jot the items down on cards. Then when it comes your way you can keep it rolling like Old Man River.

How to Be a Good Discussion Leader

A discussion without a leader is like a ship without a helmsman; it is apt to wander all over the ocean. But the discussion leader has a more exacting role than a helmsman. He does not simply steer. He is not simply a chairman. He is not a teacher or a lecturer. He is not a persuader. He is not a dictator who dominates the discussion. Instead he personifies the spirit of democracy by assisting the discussion group to work toward a solution of their problem, yet doing so without either directing or controlling their thinking.

GENERAL QUALIFICATIONS OF THE DISCUSSION LEADER

Leading a discussion is a difficult task, and frankly not everyone can handle it. But it might help to set down the general qualities needed by such a leader, if only to enable you to check them against your own abilities and know how to be on guard at those points where you may face personal difficulties.

1. *He should know the rules of the game,* should know, for example the Six Steps in Discussion, whether he is directing a Panel Forum or a Symposium Forum, when the audience is to be called on to participate, how to keep on schedule, and how to draw the ends together at the close.

2. *He should be willing to remain in the background.* "A quarterback who always elects himself to carry the ball whenever there is a chance for a touchdown will seldom be popular." A good discussion leader may indeed grow impatient, because a discussion sometimes moves slowly, but the good leader must move patiently with it, and not cut in to tell the group what's what.

3. *He should respect the opinion of others.* He may not share those opinions, but he should not let this become known to the audience. Throughout the meeting the leader gives equal opportunity to all members to express ideas. He listens to them, believing that what others think is important. He summarizes the consensus of the meeting without regard to his own personal opinions.

4. *He should be courteous, fairminded, and impartial.* A lively discussion is at times turbulent, and some of the less-controlled participants may clinch in heated arguments and resort to angry words. But the good leader never, even for an instant, loses his courteous manner. He is the moderator who not only restrains the violence of

others, but who sets an example of courteous conduct. When the argument gets hot, he breaks in with a smile and gentle hint, such as, "I think we all know how Brown and Johnson feel about this. Now who else would like to get in on it?" If a hint of this sort does not break it up, the leader can remind the group that the purpose of the discussion is to reach some solution to the problem, that the argument between the two members is preventing calm discussion, then ask these two persons to cease the argument and to permit the group to continue its discussion. A gentle admonition, courteously given by the leader, will usually quiet even the most violent member.

The good leader, above all, is fairminded and impartial. He never favors one viewpoint or restricts another. He not only permits all viewpoints to be brought out, but tries diligently to have them brought out. To persons of every viewpoint, he conveys assurance that he is a leader who plays no favorites.

The Leader's Role in Group Discussion

When asked to become the leader of a discussion group, there are certain specific tasks for which you ought to prepare:

1. *Confer in advance with other formal participants.* This will enable the leader to learn their viewpoints and to know in advance what direction the discussion is likely to take. It will also enable the leader to find out whether the other participants fully understand what is expected of them, and to make sure that each one understands the time limits of his remarks.

2. *Prepare a discussion outline.* You do not want to straitjacket the discussion by holding it to an outline prepared in advance, yet you cannot allow it to start hit-and-miss and wander whither it will. You will need to have a brief but carefully-prepared outline for use in guiding the discussion. (See page 144 for the Six Steps giving the pattern for such an outline.) Once the discussion is under way, it may suddenly turn in a wholly unexpected direction from that planned in your outline. If so, let it go the new way, so long as it is not irrelevant to the question. You may even have to make up a new outline as you go along. Very well, that is better than having no outline at the start.

3. *Open the meeting with remarks that are brief and to the point.* When a discussion group meets, it wants to get going. A leader can dull this zest and nearly kill it by long and rambling opening re-

marks. Know in advance what you are going to say. Rehearse it. Keep it short, and to the point.

4. *Keep the discussion moving.* Once the discussion is under way, it can often get stalled if the leader is not on the alert. The moment the talk begins to repeat itself, the good leader cuts off that topic and moves to the next one. If the discussion wanders from the point, he brings it back by some such remark as, "This is very interesting, but let us get back to our subject, namely. . . ." If persons with little or no information and few if any ideas try to monopolize the time (and who ever heard of a large discussion group where this did not happen?), the leader tactfully cuts them off with an explanation such as, "We have heard this member's contribution; you know, of course, that the aim of this meeting is to get everyone to participate and not to impose this burden on a few. So I know this member will now want to hear from others."

Or if the leader faces the talkative person who has strong opinions but no facts, he will ask courteously but definitely for evidence: "Now that you have stated your opinions, will you give us the evidence on which they are based?" Then if the members still insist on repeating his opinions without evidence, a tactful leader will cut in with, "Thank you very much. I think we now understand your views. Can any other member offer evidence that would give support to this opinion?" In short, the good leader keeps the ball rolling.

5. *Make occasional summaries.* After the discussion has run for awhile, or some phase of it has been completed, the leader should present a summary in order that participants can see where they now stand. Make the summaries brief and impartial. A good leader often asks the group to check him for accuracy, to make sure that he has not misstated a viewpoint, and to add points he has overlooked.

6. *Bring out all viewpoints on the subject.* Here is a high test of the leader's genius. Again and again, all the discussion will be on one side of the subject. Seemingly nobody will have an opinion on the other side. Don't be deceived. This does not always mean that nobody holds an opposite opinion. More often it means that the minority, feeling that their views are unpopular, are simply keeping quiet. A good leader *studies the faces* of the group and notes whether they seem to be in disagreement. (This requires no mind reading or mental telepathy, for people in groups show rather well in their faces whether

they are for or against an idea.) The leader then specifically invites opposing arguments, or even suggests one or two himself in order to encourage the other side to follow up. Or he may add, "I see by their faces that there are some people who hold opposing opinions. Would one of them care to state his views?"

7. *Close the meeting by a summary of the whole discussion.* Such a summary is not in the form of a set of resolutions, but is rather an attempt to state the consensus of the group. It is done with due allowance for differences of opinion, "Some believe that . . . others believe that. . . ." A good summary sends the members away with the feeling that they have got somewhere, that the discussion has helped to solve, or at least to understand, the problem involved.

Exercises

1. Listen to a radio or television discussion and report on the following: (a) Which of the Six Steps of discussion were covered. (b) Whether in your opinion any steps left out should have been covered, or any covered should have been left out. (c) How you would have discussed the problem differently if you had been a participant.

2. Assume that you are to lead a campus discussion: (a) What subject would you select? (b) What kind of discussion would you hold (Panel Forum, Symposium Forum, etc.)? (c) Whom would you invite to take part? (d) What outline of topics would you follow?

3. The class will select a topic for Cooperative Investigation, then elect a leader. The leader, of course, will lay careful plans: (a) Appoint a special committee to give the topic preliminary consideration and to divide it into subtopics (or the leader may do this himself, or in conference with others). (b) Appoint members of the class to investigate each of the subtopics. (c) Conduct the Cooperative Investigation with the entire class taking part.

4. The class will select a topic for a Panel Forum, then select a leader and four additional panel members. The leader and panel members will prepare carefully. Probably they should meet a few times and construct an outline of the points they want to cover, although each member will be left free to present his own viewpoint. Class members who are not on the panel should remember that they have parts also: both of listening carefully to the panel and of being ready to take part in the ensuing forum discussion.

5. The class will organize itself into a Legislative Assembly and set up a group of committees so that each person in the class is a member of one committee. Class members can then introduce bills into the Assembly, as many as they want. When all bills have been presented, the Assembly will

vote on which bills it wants to consider, and the Speaker of the Assembly will refer these bills to the proper committees, taking care to see that every committee has a bill referred to it. The committees will then meet and discuss the bills. This discussion, of course, ought to follow the regular Discussion Steps and ought to represent cooperative group thinking. Out of the discussion each committee will prepare a report. If committee members cannot agree on a single report, then two reports may be prepared—a majority and a minority report. The committee chairman will present the report at the next class meeting; and if there are both a minority and a majority report, another committee member can report the second one. After the bills have been reported, the Assembly can discuss them further and vote on them, but this is not necessary for the purpose of this project. The real purpose is to give committee members experience in working on a problem by thinking and talking together.

Chapter 11

ADAPTING SPEECHES TO RADIO
AND TELEVISION

On radio and television the invisible audience increases the necessity for observing basic speaking techniques, for now you must compensate for the lack of visual cues. This is true whether you speak without a studio audience or with one, for out beyond is your real audience, scattered and unseen. Consider this unseen audience for a moment. You may be talking to 50,000 people, but they are not a 50,000-size audience. They are separated into groups of twos and threes sitting comfortably in their own homes. The women perhaps are wearing house dresses; the men are smoking, perhaps with their neckties loose and feet in house slippers. Usually they are giving only half attention, meanwhile also glancing at a newspaper, talking, eating, or tinkering. If anything coming out of a radio or television seems good, they pause to decide whether it is worth the effort of careful listening, then give close attention or relax as before. They are not in a social situation, not influenced by mass presence of others, and not subject to the quickened responsiveness that characterizes the crowd.

In a public audience few people will leave the auditorium, no matter how poor the speaker. No such compulsion exists on radio and television. By a turn of the wrist a listener cuts off an uninteresting program and picks up another. He chooses what he wants to hear. He has many to choose from.

Adapting a Speech to the Radio

Few speakers can hold an unseen radio audience for more than 15 minutes. Those who can are so rare that you can count yourself out—

definitely out. Your problem is how to hold it for 15 minutes or less. The first minute or two is critical. Out across the ether in those thousands of homes you are being sized up. If you do not arrest attention and arouse lively interest, out will go several thousands of hands—and you go off the air. In a sense, a radio speech is a race between arousing interest and being cut off the air.

PLANNING THE SPEECH

The following suggestions come from persons with long radio experience:

1. *Write your talk.* For most speakers talking face-to-face with an audience extemporaneous speaking (note that we said extemporaneous speaking, not impromptu speaking) is the most effective of all modes. But not for the radio speaker. Often he does not "face" an audience at all. He faces only a cold microphone. His unseen audience cannot observe his smile, turn of body—actions that carry personal meanings to spectators. Even a long pause, which is common enough in face-to-face speaking, cannot be used on radio because it gives listeners the uneasy feeling that the radio has gone dead. Finally, a radio program is timed with what directors call "that three seconds leeway." You have no alternative but to write the speech. Indeed most radio stations will not let you in the studio until you present a manuscript.

2. *Organize the speech by a simple thought pattern.* You might want to review the discussion of thought patterns found in Chapter 6, for now you will need to apply that knowledge as never before. Avoid a complex thought pattern. You cannot watch listeners to tell whether they understand you, and if you could there is not a second of time for you to pause and clear up confusion. Therefore, for the main structure use two or three clearly related ideas, so phrased that the relationship is instantly clear.

3. *Plan to get the listener's attention at once and to hold it.* By "at once" is meant in the first sentence. Cut all wind-up. You know the ways of supporting ideas so as to hold attention. You have studied them previously: Illustrations, Specific Instances, Comparison and Contrast, Description, Narration. Use them. Make your talk vital with human-interest stories, narrative illustrations, references to events and things that are familiar in everyday life.

4. *Use simple words and short sentences.* As the Columbia Broadcasting System puts it, "Inflation, as an economic term, means little to people. But expressed as pork chops at a dollar a pound, it means an awful lot." The word "domicile" is highbrow, but "home" carries meaning to all. People like plain simple words. Use them.

Avoid long twisting sentences; make them short and straight. Remember the radio maxim that any sentence over twenty words is too long. Make yours twenty words or less, and strip the elaborate phrases and winding clauses.

Finally, make your writing sound like *talk.* Especially, use the contractions that well-bred people use in everyday speech. People simply don't say, "It is. . . ." but *"It's."* They don't say, "We do not," but *"We don't."*

5. *Give double care to transitions, summaries, and the statement of main heads.* The radio listener is deprived of those little transitions and punctuations that good speakers often give unconsciously with the head, face, hands and body. The radio speaker, therefore, must supply them with actual words. A safe precaution is to label each main topic in advance, and to summarize it tersely when finished. Throughout the speech give more than usual care to the essential connections—words like *but, also, furthermore, hence, and therefore.*

6. *Type your manuscript in readable form.* Studios recommend that speeches be double spaced on white or yellow paper (don't use crackly paper) roughly $8\frac{1}{2}$ x 11 inches in size, and spaced with a 2-inch margin all around. This makes the copy easy to read and also allows space for marginal notations.

7. *Mark your manuscript so as to help you bring out the full meaning of each thought.* This is common usage among good speakers and announcers. Each develops his personal system of markings. Some use red and green pencils, different colors for different directions. Some use single and double underlinings, and single and double pause-markings. Mark it in any way that has the most obvious meaning to you. The following reproduction shows how a typical manuscript has been marked:

Just what is a sophomore? If you believe that a dictionary can

answer all questions of definition, then open your Webster. (You

will find) that "sophomore" comes from two Greek words. (One) is SOPH-us,

meaning wise. The other is MŌ-ros, meaning fool. There is another

modern English word also derived from "moros." It is the word, "moron."

So, by definition, a sophomore is a "wise moron."

But does that definition really tell you what a sophomore is?

THE KEY

"sophomore" — the underlining means special emphasis; the quotation marks mean even more emphasis.

"really" — multiple underlinings mean terrific emphasis.

(You will find) — parenthesized phrases indicate that the voice is to be dropped.

SŌPH-us — Ō shows how the o is pronounced; capitals mean that this syllable is to be stressed.

Marking the copy will help you to read the speech so it sounds like talk. Reading so it sounds like talk is difficult, more difficult than speaking extempore, for in reading you see the words flat on the page, all typed in letters of the same size. You tend to read flat-on-the-page words in flat tones, never changing tone color, emphasis, or timing. You tend to give as much stress to tie-up words like *to*, *of*, *the* and *a*, as to the important thought-carrying words. The result is word patter, not the rhythm and stress of talk. By marking the copy you will make it easier to concentrate on ideas, to use the pause to get set for the next thought, and to construct the thought in your mind.

8. *Rehearse your talk.* In that interesting booklet published by Columbia Broadcasting System on *Making Friends with the Microphone*, the question is asked, "Don't we rehearse?" and the answer is "We certainly do." In fact, many able radio speakers do more than merely rehearse; they make an advance recording of their speech, play it back and study it for clarity, inflection, and tone quality. For beginners this ought to be compulsory. It helps them check the rate, emphasis, variety and tone color. Especially, it allows them to learn

whether they tend to "blast" the microphone with overemphasis on certain sounds, or fade out inaudibly at the end of sentences.

9. *Time your speech carefully in advance.* On the radio even a few seconds count. For example, in a 15-minute program, 30 seconds is allowed for technical station and network operation. That leaves $14\frac{1}{2}$ minutes actual speaking time. Of this, the announcer ordinarily takes about 1 minute in the opening and closing. That leaves the speaker $13\frac{1}{2}$ minutes. He must not run over and he must not run short. He must come out "on the nose."

With a manuscript in hand and the words in plain sight the tendency is to read too fast. How fast does a good radio speaker talk? That depends on the person. The average talks about 140 words a minute, with good speakers varying 10 to 25 words either way. Yet Franklin D. Roosevelt spoke at 117 words a minute, and fast-talking Walter Winchell speaks at about 215 words a minute. Do not try to talk at a predetermined rate, but use the pace that best enables you to communicate thought and feeling. Reading in this way, *time your speech, page by page, and mark the time on the bottom of each page.* Then when you broadcast the speech you can check this marked time against the studio clock (it is always visible to the radio speaker), and make sure you are talking at the rate you have planned.

FACING THE MICROPHONE

At last you are ready to give the speech. You have a manuscript. You have rehearsed it, marked it, timed it. You are now standing or sitting before the microphone and the second hand on the big studio clock is ticking toward the zero second. You get the signal. You are on the air!

In preparation for this moment, there are a few things you ought to know about facing so sensitive an instrument as the microphone:

1. *Remember that you are talking to unseen groups of only two or three persons.* No matter how many thousands are listening, they are sittings in groups of twos and threes. Don't talk to them as you would to a hundred people in an auditorium, but rather as you would talk to people sitting beside you—in your very best conversational tone.

2. *Don't raise your voice pitch.* Under the tension of speaking the tendency is to tighten the throat muscles, and thus raise the voice pitch. But on the radio a high-pitched tone sounds especially strained and affected. A quiet easy voice is best; and the most pleasant reg-

isters are the normal middle and lower tones. So relax those throat muscles and let the pitch down to its normal level. Don't be alarmed if your voice sounds a bit flat, or if the pauses seem a shade long. These are the normal effects in a room with special studio acoustics.

3. *Don't blast and fade into the microphone.* The microphone goes to both extremes in volume. If you explode a word the result will be a blast. On the other hand, if your voice falls away at the end of a sentence (this is called *dropsy* in some studios) your words will fade into inaudibility. Your voice will then come out of the loudspeaker something like this:

> Ladies and gentlemen: MMMMMMMM [unintelligible because of blast] I want to talk about today is *mmmmmm* of the *prrmmmmmm* [can't be heard because of fade].

Inequalities in volume that would pass unnoticed in an auditorium will simply ruin a radio speech. Therefore, avoid sudden sharp changes in volume. For radio emphasis, changes in intensity are better than changes in volume.

4. *Don't weave back and forth, or turn away from the microphone.* If you change the distance from your mouth to the microphone your voice will fade, boom, and distort. Keep the same distance. How far back you should stand or sit, depends on the type of microphone and on your particular voice quality. The experts in the studio will take care of that. Your responsibility is to stay put, so that an *even* tone goes into the microphone.

5. *Keep all other noises out of the microphone.* What other noises, you may wonder, can get into a microphone in a soundproof studio? The answer is noises that you make.

First, don't clear your throat, smack your lips, cough into the microphone, tap a pencil, drum on the table, or snap your fingers. These are high-pitched sounds that often crack like a pistol shot in the ears of those far-off listeners. If you must cough, turn your face away and bury it deep in a handkerchief. If such a cough gets into the microphone anyhow, apologize, so listeners will know you are not a boor. A simple, "Sorry," or "I beg pardon," is enough to let the listeners know you are not wantonly "coughing in their faces."

Second, avoid rustling the pages of your manuscript. To the listener crackling paper sounds like hail on a tin roof. A good procedure is to make a final check just before you go on the air to see that your pages are in proper order, then remove the paper clip (never speak with a manuscript clipped together). As you finish with each page, simply let that sheet fall to the table or floor. You have thus got rid of it without the chance of a rustle.

Third, breathe silently. This advice might tempt you to protest, "What? Can't I even breathe in peace before a microphone?" That depends on how you breathe. A sudden intake is magnified by the microphone into a whistle. So keep relaxed and breathe silently and deep.

Fourth, keep your hands off the microphone. Avoid that temptation to "stroke it, tickle it, pat it, tap it, and climb it." These aimless little efforts produce sounds like an artillery bombardment.

Finally, say absolutely nothing for at least fifteen seconds before and after you are on the air. That microphone might be open! You can't tell by looking at it! There was once a man who thought he was off the air, and so he said to the announcer, . . . But maybe you heard about that one. Don't let it happen to you.

Adapting a Speech to Television

Planning and writing a television speech is the same as for radio, except that in television you may want to add the use of visual aids. But facing a television camera is markedly different from facing only a microphone. The speaker's face, clothes, the way he wears his necktie, and the manner of the man himself—or the woman—all assume cumulative significance. The speaker must conform both to the limitations of the microphone and to the television camera, in which the latter requires movement, yet restricts the area of movement. Techniques are not yet fully explored but the following represents their present development:

1. *Consider the possibilities of visual aids.* A basic requirement of television is *variety,* for listeners will not look at an unchanging image on the screen for ten minutes, or even two. Therefore every available technique is used for making seemingly natural changes of image on the screen. One of these available to you as a speaker is visual aids—maps, charts, diagrams, models, slides, and films. Sometimes, especially with maps and charts and diagrams, they are placed beside you or just behind you, so you can point to them or mark them with a large visible crayon as you talk. Or they may be located a few

feet away where you can step over to them while talking. Materials that you do not need to explain by pointing can be set up at some distance, to be picked up by another camera. Slides and films, of course, are handled from the projection booth.

2. *Find out in advance where you will stand or sit, and how far you may move without getting outside the camera range or depth of focus.* The size of image is determined by distance to the camera and by the focal length of the lens being used. By changing the distance and changing the lens the cameras can shift the image from face-only to waist-up, and distant-view including background scenery or visual aids. Also, photographs are made from different angles—front, side, above, below—and to give variety, changes will be made in both angles and distances while you are speaking. Almost always two cameras are used, but if only one is used it will be tilted, swung from side to side, or moved in and out.

The studio will instruct you as a matter of procedure about staying within camera range and focus, but you will want to arrange for placing your manuscript so it will not be conspicuous; and if visual aids are used you will want to know in advance how they are to be located, and where is the best position for you to stand in explaining them.

You don't want to appear conscious of the camera while speaking, yet mentally you should keep track of which camera is picking you up, and should adapt your movements to its angle. (You can know this easily because at the bottom of the camera small red lights turn on when it goes into action.)

3. *Learn about clothes and make-up that give best effect.* The television camera has a high response to infra-red rays which changes the appearance of clothes and gives the effect of seeing beneath the skin. The older cameras, for example, made tuxedo lapels look gray, and some figured dresses look as though an egg had been smeared on them. The normal reddish color of the lips disappeared, freshly shaven men had that "five o'clock shadow," clean faces appeared to be dirty, and the natural shadows of the face looked unnatural. They do better now; both cameras and lighting have been improved. Even so, be careful. Formerly you had to avoid either black or white, especially white shirts. Shirts of pale blue, tan, gray, and eggshell were all right, but not white. Now you can wear white shirts in most studios, but must still be careful of other contrasts, for the television cameras will not handle the contrasts some people wear in everyday life, and it

makes a little contrast go a long way. A gray pinstripe suit and a gray shirt, for example, may look almost the same color to the human eye, but not on television; there it will show up in pleasing contrast.

To avoid bizarre effects you had best inquire what clothes to wear. Especially also, watch jewelry and shining objects. Assuredly on the television screen all that glitters is not gold. Beads, rings, pins, earrings, and even bald heads will also glitter dazzlingly.

4. *Don't let the manuscript come between you and the audience.* Handling notes or manuscript is the most difficult adjustment a speaker has to make for television speaking. As on the radio your speech needs to be timed close to that "three seconds leeway," hence you need one carefully prepared. Unlike radio, you can't read it outright, for obviously it is disastrous for a television audience to see only the top of your head, or to see it constantly bobbing up and down over a manuscript.

There is no easy way around the problem; whichever way you go is rough. Memorizing is seldom the answer, for most memorized speeches *sound* memorized. So speakers and commentators are meeting the problem in other ways:

(1) Most public officials still use a manuscript and read it badly. The listeners endure it because of the person's official position. Unless you hold public office, this method is out.

(2) Others use a manuscript, but have it so well in mind that they merely *glance* at it at moderate intervals. They seem almost to be speaking without notes, and actual stopwatch timing shows them to be looking at the audience at least 90 per cent of the time. With their manuscript glances trimmed to 10 per cent or less of speaking time, they maintain excellent audience contact. Some of this group keep almost verbatim to the words on the manuscript. Others use the copy for thought guidance, and follow a semi-*ad-lib* method.

(3) Some speakers now use a teleprompter. (Arthur Godfrey and many other television performers use one.) A teleprompter is a box, some 18 inches square, concealed from the camera and the live audience, but visible to the speaker. The copy is typed on a roll in very large letters, inserted in the teleprompter, and illuminated so as to throw the heavy lettering into relief. As the speaker proceeds, the roll moves from bottom to top with six or eight lines always visible.

DWIGHT EISENHOWER

In a telecast speech he is using large cards instead of a teleprompter.

Usually a person below deck controls the speed and varies it to allow for applause or other interruptions.

(4) News commentators often use a half-notes-half-memorized system. They memorize the basic features of each story, then for the telecast set up large cards near the camera on which they put leads of four or five words, or a list of topics. Then they speak extempore, but follow the memorized sequence of each story. When looking at the cards, of course, they seem to be looking at the camera.

(5) A few speakers, including Dwight Eisenhower, adopt the method developed by shows like *We the People* for handling programs that are only slightly rehearsed. It consists of putting the entire speech on huge cards, about 3x5 feet, with about eight lines per card. These cards are placed beside a camera so the speaker seems to be looking into the camera as he reads the speech.

6. *Converse directly and intimately as though to a small group.* A telecast speech is an intimate conversation. The camera's electronic eye almost literally goes beneath the surface when it makes the picture. The audience is seated in small groups. The screen is small compared with the great silver screen of moving pictures. Everything lends itself to the illusion of closeness. Speak, therefore, as though you were talking to a small group earnestly face-to-face. Remember that television is no place for a high-pressure speaking tone or excited manner. These give the effect of your trying to push the listeners around, and their response will be "quit pushing."

7. *Adapt your action to close-up speaking.* Television restores much of the eye communication so conspicuously missing on radio. But action on television is not identical with action in an auditorium. It is more like the best action in private conversation. In an auditorium you need extended action—a sweep of the arm, large movements of the body—for people to see at a distance. On television such extended action is overdone; it marks you as a "ham." More often than not on television, you do not stand up and speak formally, but are seated at a desk, as in an office, or even in an easy chair, as at home. This is a new kind of posture. You don't want to sit stiff-backed, but rather to sit as in alert, friendly conference. Thus far you can be merely "natural" if your natural manner in private conversation is good enough. But from this point on, you cannot be "natural." You must adopt a technique that gives the *illusion* of naturalness. For example, in private conversation you might sit for a minute or two

without deliberately changing posture. Not on television. On that screen you must have variety, and to have it you need deliberately to change posture with reasonable frequency—and do it so you give the illusion of doing it naturally. You may lean forward to emphasize an idea, turn your body or nod your head to mark a transition. You may explain, describe, locate, and differentiate ideas with your hands —not with extended action, but in reduced form as though talking to people sitting beside you. You will look at the camera, and look away. You will consciously seek variety that looks natural, attempting an art that conceals art.

Finally, watch your mannerisms. Many of us are guilty of trick manners, facial contortions, wasted motions, and repetition of action, which we usually don't know about. Our friends are used to them, and are less distracted by them than are strangers. But such mannerisms don't go well on television. The illusion of closeness on the screen magnifies them. They distract and even irritate those who are not our friends.

Assuredly this does not mean for you to give up the hallmarks of your own personality and try to be a robot. Good television speaking rather demands that you intensify personality. But it also demands that you get rid of annoying mannerisms. On this you cannot check yourself. You need the advice of others who watch you rehearse.

Exercises

1. Listen to a good radio speaker and report on what you think are the factors of his effectiveness. Include manner of speaking, articulation, speech content, manner of organization, and use of language.

2. Listen to a good television speaker. (a) Report on the things you *saw* that contributed to his effectiveness. (b) To focus on the technique of action. count how often the speaker changed his position or posture during a 3-minute period. (c) Count the number of camera changes, of distance and angle, made during a 3-minute period.

3. Recast one of your previous speeches in this course so it will be adapted for radio broadcast.

4. Recast one of your previous speeches in this course for telecasting. With marginal notes indicate what visual aids you would use. Also indicate special adaptations of posture and movement you would use.

5. Write out and record a 1-minute newscast. Remember that the announcer's problem of reading aloud is like the actor's. He must *seem* natural, but

cannot *be* natural. In everyday speech, sounds are often slurred and final phrases lost. If you talked in this "natural"way over the microphone, without the aid of gestures and sight, your voice simply would not make sense. An announcer, like an actor, must overdo to seem natural. The good announcer overdoes just enough to make it seem natural, whereas the "ham" overdoes in a way that seems overdone.

6. Write out and record a 3-minute radio speech:

    a. Type the manuscript, double spaced, and mark it for reading.

    b. Time it carefully; and to make sure of not running over, cut it to 2 minutes 50 seconds. *Do not* write a 3½ minute speech then try to speed it up to 3 minutes, for the faster you read the less listeners comprehend. If you have a 3½ minute speech, read it in 3 minutes, and the listener gets 1½ minutes worth, that is poor economy.

    c. Above all, be earnest; talk directly to your unseen listeners.

Chapter **12**

LISTENING EFFICIENTLY

Nearly a century ago a brilliant English scholar, Sir Richard Jebb, investigated how the oldest form of mass communication—public address—got its start. It took centuries before the first condition was met, namely that people had to give up the notion of "natural oratory" and recognize that speeches must be prepared "in accordance with the theory" of public address. Two further conditions were also necessary: First, the people had to develop government according to law, where every citizen had an equal right to speak his mind about public affairs, where both sides of a public question were fairly heard and were decided by the opinion of the majority. Finally, and perhaps foremost, there had to be "popular intelligence," "a paramount People, taught by life to reason and to judge." [1]

In other words, man's earliest means of mass communication became possible, not solely because people learned how to prepare speeches " in accordance with the theory." That was only part of the process. Before there could really be mass communication, the "paramount People" had to be willing and able to *listen* intelligently, then "to reason and to judge."

Obviously, unless people listen efficiently there is not much point in giving speeches, for the system of communication simply breaks down. All of this has been known, of course, for twenty-five centuries, but during most of that time people took listening for granted. "Anybody can listen," was the accepted maxim. This, of course, was a perfect parallel to that other lame half-truth, that "anybody can talk." The ancient Greeks had disproved that myth twenty-five centuries ago by discovering that effective formal public address required a theory—like painting, sculpture, or surgery. They had

[1] R. C. Jebb, *Attic Orators* (London: Macmillan and Co., 1876), cviii-cxi, cxxxii. cxxxvii.

165

developed the theory, and so became the first people to use public address as an effective mode of mass communication.

But the maxim that "anybody can listen" was not actively questioned until after the invention of radio. There was good enough reason. In the four hundred years following the invention of the printing press our educational system gave primacy to reading and writing. Literacy itself was measured in terms of reading, not listening. Suddenly, after four hundred years, radio (without the aid of television which came later) overthrew the supremacy of the written word. People now listened far more than they read. Radio, the research showed, was more effective than print, and face-to-face speaking was more effective than radio.

At first we continued to assume that "anybody could listen," that efficient listening was determined by merely hearing acuity and intelligence, and that schools could do little about either. Again, research showed this to be wrong. We had long known that efficient reading did not depend solely on eyesight and intelligence, but required training in techniques. So, it was found, with listening. Even ear-minded people do not listen at highest efficiency without training. The very people so greatly influenced by what they heard, often did not adequately understand what they heard, and thought it was something else. One careful test of college freshmen listening to professors face-to-face in short information lectures showed that "on the average listeners comprehended but 68 per cent of the material tested." Another test of 1100 persons listening to short radio speeches found that the average comprehension score was only 28 per cent.[2] In a free society that rests on "popular intelligence," and "a paramount People, taught by life to reason and to judge," this is a dangerously low display of mass comprehension.

Why is it that people, who have been listening all their life, do it so poorly? The answer that most of their listening has been done to private conversation. There listening is a single-thought, hook-and-eye process, easy to handle. But listening to a formal speech is something else. Here listeners must weave together hundreds of single-thought, hook-and-eye units into a large complex thought pattern. Hence people who listen efficiently to conversation may not listen efficiently at all to the sustained thought sequence of a formal speech. For this they need training, just as they needed training in learning to read.

[2] Ralph G. Nichols, "Factors in Listening Comprehension," *Speech Monographs*, XV (1948), No. 2, pp. 154-163; and K. A. Harwood, "Research Notes," *Journal of Communication*, II (1952), No. 2, p. 14.

You belong to a generation that presumably has been taught to read. You were born too soon for the educational system to have caught up with the world and to have set up a curriculum that taught you to listen. This chapter will attempt to give you the chance to cover that deficiency.

In the classroom you are in a favored position. You will hear a hundred or more speeches, each offering opportunity for applying the techniques of critical listening. This amounts really to a listening laboratory.

Actually, there are *two* kinds of listenings you ought to do. First, is listening to get meanings. This is the listening skill that everyone needs to develop.

Second, is listening to evaluate speech communication techniques. Most of you will take only one such course before going into a world where your usefulness to society—and your personal success—will depend in large measure on your ability to communicate ideas orally. What you get out of this one course will do more to determine how effectively you live, and how successfully in a material sense, than what you get out of almost any other course you take in college; for in a large measure it will determine how effectively you *use* what you learn in other courses. As one business man put it: "One semester or one term of superficial training in speech is not enough. He [the student] needs more than a superficial orientation. The entire field of speech, logical thinking, discussion, debate, conducting meetings must be incorporated into and made a vital part of the total education. . . . His technical training cannot be of maximum effectiveness until he has been provided with a means of communicating it to other people." [3]

You can read this textbook, take the examinations, and find out how much you have learned about speaking techniques. You can give five or ten speeches attempting to put those techniques into operation, look over the instructor's grades and comments, and see where you have succeeded or have failed. You can thereby make progress. But if you would make maximum progress, you will listen critically to every speech given by every other student, and will evaluate his use of speaking techniques. Instead of five or ten opportunities for learning techniques, you will have a hundred or more.

Your role while others speak then, is not to fade into a coma and be merely aware of sound. It is not to be half conscious, dully skim

---

[3] W. E. Bennett, Coordinator of Training, Cities Service Refining Corporation, "Speech in a Technological Society," *Journal of Communication*, I (May, 1951), No. 1, p. 19.

what is said, and rouse yourself when there is a pause, change of pace, an emphatic word, or an interesting tidbit. If you listen that way, opportunity once gone is gone forever. Rather, when others speak you are in position to say, "Here is the chance to learn without making mistakes, or having to pay for them." As each speech is given you do those *two* kinds of listening.

First, you want the answer to *"What* did the speaker say?" That is, you listen to get the idea and determine its worth: What is the speaker talking about? What is his central idea? What is his skeleton of supporting ideas? Are his facts accurate? Can his judgment be trusted? Can the speaker himself be trusted? Or is he a half-concealed propagandist?

Second, you want the answer to *"How* did the speaker say it?" That is, you listen to discover and evaluate his speaking techniques: Was he too slow getting to the point? Did he make the central idea clear? Did he state it too soon, or too late? Should he have used a summary on that topic? Would not an illustration or comparison have made that point clearer? If he talked louder would listeners have got more? If he had used action in explaining that would it have been clearer? He made that point crystal clear in two minutes; I wonder if I can use that method in my next speech? He certainly knows how to use illustrations; ought I to look into how to use them better? Note how he drove that topic home with suspense; that's where I fell down on my last speech.

Levels of Listening

There are at least five levels of listening. Literate listeners at different times use each of them. Semi-literate listeners use only the three lowest. In ascending order of difficulty these five levels are:

1. *Listening for entertainment.* This is listening merely for enjoyment to funny stories and interesting talk. It is the kind of listening we do to variety shows on radio and television. It is the kind of listening we do at popular moving picture shows.

2. *Listening for escape or sublimation.* Men like to listen to sportscasts. Women like soap operas. They let us escape from the humdrum of daily life. They epitomize our wishes and ambitions in the stories of other people. For a moment in the imagination we become Superman or Cinderella, and can live in an unreal world. Listening for escape allows a release for our wishful thinking.

3. *Listening for inspiration.* We listen also for renewing faith, for an uplift of spirit, for an inspiration to be better and do more. Sermons and religious music, inspiring drama, patriotic themes, all are founded on the human quest for inspiration.

4. *Listening for information and ideas.* Sometimes we listen for information only. This generally is the type of listening done, or at least attempted, in classroom lectures, explanations of technical subjects and new discoveries, and newscasts. We want to know what is to be known, to keep up with the world. At other times we want to have the meaning of facts explained to us. At still others we want ideas on problems that face us. In short, this type of listening is a search for facts and a quest for ideas.

5. *Listening to evaluate and form opinions.* Most listening on controversial subjects is done with a closed mind. We listen, not for facts or ideas or to form opinions, but simply to ratify old beliefs. Nevertheless, some people can listen critically, to weigh and judge and modify old opinions. Not all can do it, or want to do it. They prefer to listen only for entertainment, or for escape into a dream world, or to gain pleasure from hearing what they already believe. Some try to listen critically, but get tired after a few minutes and give up. They have not been trained to listen literately, and they go through life listening only at lower levels. Critical listening is not learned in a day. It is cultivated by slow degrees.

Obviously the kinds of listening we are henceforth concerned with are the last two levels: listening for information and ideas, and listening to evaluate and form opinions. The third level, listening for inspiration, is useful indeed; but you can learn it easily once you have acquired efficiency in the final two.

The Listening Process

Before considering specific listening techniques we should examine the nature and limitations of listening.

Listening is instantaneous. In reading you can stop and ponder. You can reread. In listening there is no backtracking. A skillful speaker will help you by repetitions and summaries, but no full re-hearing is possible. Therefore, you get it straight the first time, or you don't get it straight at all. Hence an active intelligent mind that gets meanings instantly will have about the same efficiency in listening

170   SPEECH COMMUNICATION

as in reading. But if the mental activity is lowered, a reader can compensate by rereading, whereas the listener is passed by and left behind.

In listening you can get meanings from voice and action that cannot be given you by print. From a competent speaker, a listener can get meanings that no reader can get from print. These come from the speaker's color of voice, informing inflection, pause, emphasis, and by action that points, describes, divides, discriminates. Talk is older than print. Man has evolved a code of meaning by action, a sign language, that is understood over all the world. He has also evolved an exact and subtle code of meaning by voice inflection, stress, and rhythm which is far older than any words in the English language. Print is a newcomer. It offers mere black on white. It cannot carry as full meanings as effective talk.

But the typical self-made speaker does not use these techniques. The listener may be borne toward a state of coma, or even hypnotic drowsiness, by the dripping of a dull flat voice. He may have the thought flow broken by *ahs* and *ers*, and by action that distracts or misleads. Yet under motivation, listeners, in reasonable measure, can compensate for poor delivery. They can get more out of a poorly-delivered speech than might be supposed. But it takes strong and constant motivation.

Efficient listening depends on (1) attitude, (2) attention, (3) retention, and (4) evaluation. Here we are summarizing the complicated process that goes on in a listener's mind. Consider first the effect of *attitude.* Research shows that strongly opinionated listeners learn less than others. Those who tend strongly to disagree or agree also fail more than others to get the speaker's central idea and to form valid inferences. Apparently such people spend their listening time in rationalizing their own fixed views rather than in opening their minds to the opinions of the speaker. In a sense they are not listeners. Those who strongly disagree tend to become disputers. Those who strongly agree tend to become nonthinking applauders.[4]

Attention means that you take an active part. Note the word "active." Many people think of listening as merely *receiving* communication from someone who is giving it. This is partly right, but

[4] For a summary of research the above two paragraphs see James I. Brown, "The Objective Measurement of Listening Ability," *Journal of Communication,* I (May, 1951), No. 1, pp. 45-46.

then they make the error of assuming that communication is like receiving a gift or a judgment from the court. Not so. Listening is not passive, but active. It is a different kind of activity from speaking, but it is an activity. It is more like the activity of catching a baseball. You don't wait for the ball to hit you. You reach out and gather it in. If you don't do this actively, the ball bounces off or goes on past. Listening is like catching a ball in still another way. It requires skill, a know-how. But listening is unlike catching a ball in one respect; you either catch the whole ball or miss it, whereas in listening you can catch merely a piece of the thought. Nevertheless, the analogy is a good one. Listening is like catching a ball. You get set, watch the windup, follow the throw. This calls for attention. You watch the speaker, watch his face and action, get each point as he delivers it, and relate the point to the material he delivers in support of it.

Next is *retention*. Listening is not efficient unless you remember the main lines of thought. To continue the baseball comparison, you keep track of the innings, the number of strikes, balls, outs, and the total score.

Finally, is *evaluation*. Here the baseball comparison no longer holds, for in baseball an out is an out, a score is a score, and the umpire's decision is final. Not so with listening. In a way, you make up your own score, and it may be a different score from those made up by others. It depends on your intelligence, understanding of the subject, previous attitude toward it, and listening ability. Before evaluating, you must first be able to say, *"I understand."* Until you do understand, evaluation is folly. But once you do understand, then you talk back—silently, of course. You say, "I understand, and agree." Or "I understand, and agree with reservations or modifications." Or "I understand, and suspend judgment until I can think further." Or "I understand, and disagree, for your analysis was unsound, . . . or your reasoning was fallacious, . . . or your evidence was rigged." In this way you sift, measure, and judge. You place one fact against another, one judgment against another, and emerge with a concept that is a fusion of material already in your mind plus new ones delivered by the speaker.

Evaluation calls for the highest skill in listening. Some listeners fail in the essential first step; they do not *understand* what the speaker says, hence the evaluation is worth little. Other listeners are efficient on pure reception of details, but have trouble combining these details into a thought pattern, or in judging their relevancy. Finally, there are those undisciplined minds found in every class who are propelled almost entirely by prejudices. Often mentally rude, and often insensitive to the responses of others, their prejudices to them are the Voice of God, and rational judgment is the Whisper of the Serpent. Such people cannot evaluate. They can only dispute.

How to Listen Effectively

From this background we can set down six steps in the technique of efficient listening:

1. *Get ready to listen.* Have you observed how some people like to sit at the back of the room, or near an exit where outside noises mask the speaker's voice? Have you seen a student enter a classroom, and slouch down in a seat, feet out and head back? Such people seldom listen efficiently. Many, in fact, do not come to listen efficiently. In getting ready to listen, seat yourself where you can see and hear, take a comfortable but alert posture, focus your eyes on the speaker and your mind on what he is about to say.

2. *Switch off emotional attitudes.* We already know what research has found about attitudes. People with strong emotional attitudes don't listen well. Not only do they fail to make relevant judgments, but they even fail to get the speaker's central idea. You cannot listen efficiently when strong emotions are chasing themselves through your mind, when you are saying mentally, "Of course he's right; any fool could see that," or "There's nothing to be said on his side of the question," or "I wish I were not stuck with this assignment." You cannot yield to emotional attitudes and at the same time listen efficiently. The emotions win, and listening comes in a poor second. Therefore, switch off emotional attitudes.

3. *Start listening on the first sentence.* You can reread printed matter, but you hear a speaker's words only once. If you don't get them straight the first time, you don't get them—period. Good speakers often state the central idea in the first minute or so, or even the first few seconds. If you miss the central idea, you will have trouble through the speech in getting the thought pattern. Start listening, then, on the first sentence. If it is mere windup, let it pass, but keep set for the statement of the central idea, or for definitions, ground clearing

or orientation of any sort. That first minute or so is critical. After that listening becomes a little easier.

4. *Get the central idea.* Every speech worth listening to has a unity, and an organization of parts. Find, first, the unity, the central idea. If the speaker does not put it into exact words, do so yourself. If, when the speech is over, you can't state briefly what the theme was, you have not listened efficiently. You may have a lot of interesting details, but the speech will be what William James said the world is to a baby: "a big, buzzing, blooming confusion."

5. *Get the chief supporting ideas in their relation to the whole.* A speech, like a human being, has a skeleton that holds it erect. This skeleton, like the human skeleton, is covered up with muscles and dressed up in clothes. Your job is to X-ray through clothes and muscles to find the skeleton. You can then see what kind of creature the speech is, how it hangs together, and how its parts are articulated. In other words, a speech is a *complex* unity. You have not grasped its complex unity if you know only its central idea. You must know also its major parts, how they are organized into a whole, and how they are organically related.

To borrow an analogy from Mortimer Adler,[5] a good speech is like a good house. It is under one roof, but has different rooms on different levels, and the rooms are used for different purposes. In a degree each room is independent, each having its own structure and interior design. Yet no room is totally independent and separate; they are connected by corridors, stairways, arches, and doors; and the special use of each room contributes to the total usefulness of the house. A speech, like a house, has an orderly design of parts. Each major part has a degree of independence, each has its own interior structure and design. Yet no part is totally independent and separate from the others. Each is connected by passageways called transitions; and the special contribution of each part contributes to the total usefulness of the speech.

You may say this looks as though it were a rule of speaking instead of listening. So it is. Speaking and listening are reciprocal. If speakers do not organize their ideas, if they fail to present a central idea and an orderly skeleton of parts, there would be no point in the listener's search for unity and for uncovering structure. For that matter, there would not be much point in speaking, or in listening.

[5] *How to Read a Book* (New York: Simon and Schuster, 1940), p. 164.

A skillful speaker helps you get the major parts, their relation to each other, and their relation to the whole. Watch for the cue phrases as "First," or "At the beginning." They tell you that here comes the first major part. Then watch for cue phrases like "another consideration," or "Second," which tell you that the speaker is now coming to the second major part. If you have trouble at first in carrying these parts in your mind, write them down. A little practice in writing down the major parts will help soon to carry them in your head.

Watch also the cues the speaker gives you at the end of a major part. He may wrap it up, round it out, or even summarize it: "What I have been saying, then, amounts to this," or "To put it another way," or "In summary."

Especially watch the summary that comes at the end of the speech. Here you have a chance to get a bird's-eye view of all the speaker has said, and to pick up points and relationships you missed the first time.

6. *Weigh and consider*. So far we have been talking about reception, getting clearly what the speaker says, so with reasonable certainty you can say, "I understand." ". . . And with all thy getting get understanding." Now comes the final end of listening: evaluating what you understand. You can pronounce any sort of judgment— biased, bickering, undisciplined; or reflective, relevant, mature. You can make no effort to evaluate, but simply forget it. You can damn with faint praise, then put it aside. You can reject without judgment. But assuming an ability for critical judgment, or a willingness to develop it—you can undertake the final step of criticism, judgment, and evaluation. Criticism, of course, is not disagreement. It is not listening in order to doubt or to scorn. It is evaluating under the terms so well stated in Francis Bacon's recommendation to readers: "Read not to contradict or confute; not to believe and take for granted; nor to find talk and discourse; but to weigh and consider."

Exercises

1. Test first your ability to listen for information. Your instructor will read a 3-minute article from *Time*, *Newsweek*, etc. Take no notes during the reading, but immediately afterward write a brief summary stressing only important items.

2. Listen to a public speech (on radio or television if you prefer) and write a report on: (a) the speaker's central idea, (b) the chief supporting ideas, (c) your evaluation of them.

3. In listening to the next round of class speeches, evaluate the speaking techniques of each speaker. Which were well used? Which poorly used? Which were ignored?

4. Draw up a list of the factors that make it difficult for you to listen efficiently. Prepare your next speech with these factors in mind, taking special care to prepare and deliver the speech so these missing cues are given your listeners. Attach your list of factors to the outline. On the left margin of the outline explain the methods you plan to use for giving special cues to the listeners.

Appendix

SPECIMEN SPEECHES

ROADS TO AGREEMENT

By *Stuart Chase*

You will recall that students were advised to avoid argument and controversy in their first speeches, and to learn the fundamentals of giving interesting speeches of information (page 29). Stuart Chase's speech does exactly that. At half a dozen places where a less skillful speaker would provoke argument, he deftly avoids it and keeps strictly to "a speech to inform." Yet this "speech to inform" stimulates listeners to think, and perhaps even do something about improving the roads to agreement. If you want to know why, check the techniques in this speech against those discussed in Chapter 8, on Persuasion. Note especially that the speaker: (1) Uses all of the five techniques of Getting and Holding Attention (humor is least used, but there are mild flashes of it). (2) Quickly leads listeners to believe that the speaker knows what he is talking about, and hence to "accept his competence." (3) Develops the speech by carefully organized information that rests on the listeners' wants, hopes, and aspirations—especially those of Survival, Security, and the Desire to Be a Part of Something Worthwhile. In short, here is a pure "speech to inform" that by skillful planning becomes in the long run a speech to persuade.

It was given at the 18th Biennial Congress of the Cooperative League of the U.S.A., in Chicago, November 6, 1952. Stuart Chase is well known for his 25 books on economic problems, semantics, and on applying the scientific method to human relations.

Armed with what might be called a reportorial walkie-talkie, I recently set out to collect techniques of agreement from anyone in any place that could show me a dependable method for reducing conflict and aiding agreement. I visited universities, personnel departments, union headquarters, management conferences, laboratories, clinics, Quaker business meetings, UNESCO, the TVA, the National Planning Association, the Foreign Service Institute of the State Department, Mr. Cyrus Ching.

After Hiroshima this inventory seemed a useful undertaking. We may or may not be our brothers' keepers, but with jet propulsion and other products of applied science, we are increasingly in our brothers' laps. Anyone who can help us get along together better in this shrinking space is a benefactor of the race. We can't afford quarrels we used to enjoy before $E=MC^2$ broke loose.

I identified at least 18 varieties of conflict, from a row between two people to the gigantic East versus West conflict which now shakes the planet. They can be arranged into a kind of skyscraper with a fight on each floor. To gaze up at it is both impressive and depressing. How can it ever be bypassed?

Fortunately there are three major offsets to conflict which should never be lost sight of. Some first class work by social scientists recently has emphasized their importance.

176

1. Conflict is often due to a cause other than the apparent one. Frustration and insecure people, people afraid, are far more likely to pick quarrels than well adjusted and secure people. Look at the Middle East right now. Frustration leads to aggression.

2. Man is a social animal and must have a community around him at least peaceful enough to rear his young—a long process—and teach them to talk, failing which they cannot think.

3. Any human society is, and must be, a vast network of mutual agree-ments. Without them "all of us would be huddling in miserable and lonely caves not daring to trust anyone." The network is, of course, the culture which we begin to learn as soon as we are born. Our interdependence is well illustrated by the dictum: "Your liberty to swing your arms ends where my nose begins."

Thus below all the conflicts which divide individuals, families, regions, political parties, religious sects, lies this broad foundation of common agree-ment due to a shared culture.

With those three general offsets to the skyscraper as a starter, I proceeded to collect specific techniques of agreement. There are, you will be glad to hear, a vast number of them. Here are some samples from my inventory which particularly illustrate cooperative behavior.

I

One of the roads to agreement which particularly fascinated me was group dynamics—a study of the energy locked up in people which can be released only through appropriate group action.

The Quakers in their business meetings have amply verified the value of group study—a verification extending over three centuries. They know how to pool the experience of members, study solutions of a problem which no in-dividual member had previously thought of, and reach *unanimous* agree-ment. They avoid voting, so there is no majority to crow and no minority to feel sore.

I factored out nine principles from a Quaker meeting. Some tie into modern studies of group behavior, and all bear on classroom education. Besides una-nimity, the Quaker principles include: participation and involvement of members in problems and solutions; careful listening—a technique alien to most Americans; periods of silence to delay emotional responses; "per-missive" leaders; equality of status for all members; priority of facts over opinions; a moratorium for questions which stir emotions and cause sides to form. The question whether members of the Philadelphia Meeting should own slaves came up for decades. The unanimous answer was no, in 1776—85 years before the Civil War!

Here is a case from England. After World War II so many returned officers stormed Oxford and Cambridge that the ancient tutorial system broke down. Tutors, instead of taking on one boy at a time, were forced to take on five or six. To everyone's surprise, it was found that students learned more by group study than alone. "There is a distinct gain in meeting more than one student," says a Rockefeller Foundation report by Robert T. Crane. "Students engage in mutual discussion, often continued beyond the session with the tutor." In group discussion the subject has a better chance of coming alive.

Ski instructors find that private lessons are less effective for the learners than group lessons. Says *The String Player:* "Violin students should be taught in groups. Children not only derive a great deal of pleasure from this approach, but they learn much more rapidly by watching one another, hearing one another, and by making comparisons. . . . The strong points of the student should be emphasized in front of the class in order to build confidence." *Per contra* weak points should *not* be emphasized, as this compounds the embarrassment.

How do some people settle wars and reach agreements? Here are some cases on the labor front. I set up my walkie-talkie at many places along that front and most of the results are very encouraging.

How did Cyrus Ching settle disputes? Shortly before he resigned as head of the Federal Mediation Service, I backed Mr. Ching into a corner of his office one day in Washington to find out how he did it. I discovered he didn't know how he did it. He had no set rule or plan to follow—he plays by ear. However, my questioning aroused his curiosity. He said: "When I retire I am going to see if I can't jot down some of the principles which I have been following."

Going from Washington to Cambridge—at M.I.T. I found Joseph Scanlon, ex-union official and now a full time professor at M.I.T. His job is a very interesting one for an engineering school. When I was at M.I.T. we did not do anything like that. His job is to go around visiting industrial firms who invite him to come in and settle their labor-management situations, setting up participation plans between union and management representatives for increasing production. He won't go in unless the plant has a union, and he takes graduate students along with him so they may learn something about human relations in industry. The union takes an active part in reducing costs, increasing efficiency and morale. To date he has set up over 40 plans and they have been written up in *Fortune* and elsewhere. I would like to tell you very briefly about Scanlon and his participation plan. I can see him in his office now, describing to me how it all started. I think you will agree with me that it was a dramatic beginning.

Scanlon, at that time, was a young cost accountant in a steel mill not far from Pittsburgh. The depression struck and the situation got worse and worse and then a union came in—the C.I.O. Steel Workers. Scanlon resigned his job as cost accountant and went down and took a job on the bench and presently became the leader of the local union. As the depression deepened the mill headed towards the rocks. The president of the company and the other top officials wanted desperately to keep going. They all had their salaries cut drastically but the sheriff was pretty close to the door.

Joe Scanlon called a meeting of the union. He stationed his largest members at the door to act as guards so nobody could get out and he laid the facts about the mill on the table before the union. As an accountant, he knew what the actual financial situation was. He told the union members that the mill

was really in desperate straits. He told them about the president and officers—
that they were just as frightened as the men were. Where were the men going
to get new jobs if the mill closed down? The nearest possibility of any jobs
was in Pittsburgh, and there were plenty of bread lines forming there. The
men had never heard this before. Finally it dawned on them that they could
take a three months' wage cut of 25% in an attempt to save the mill.

They formed and set up a production committee with representatives from
labor and management. Scanlon was elected head of that committee. The committee went to work and pretty soon costs came down. The mill eventually
went from the red into the black and in due course the 25% cut was paid
back and at last accounts the mill was still going strong.

Then we have, again on the labor-management front, a very interesting five
year study of the National Planning Association, not into industrial trouble
but into industrial peace. The NPA sent out field workers to industrial plants
with good management relations to find out the principles on which those
companies operated. Indeed I have noticed tremendous progress on this front
since I worked with the Labor Bureau back in the 1920's. Of course, there
are still far too many strikes, but not nearly as many as there were then and
also not nearly so violent. This is where human relations comes in. For instance, nowadays what does a steel company do when they have a strike?
They send out hot coffee to the picket lines!

II

The usual result of classes in English composition, says S. I. Hayakawa,
author of *Language in Thought and Action,* is not competent writing but a
lifelong terror of grammatical mistakes. Freshman themes are literary ship-
wrecks, not because the student is stupid, but because an assignment is
meaningless to him; his interest is not involved.

Hayakawa's method is to let freshmen write, not for the teacher, but for
each other! They choose a subject they wish to explain to the class. The ditto
machines and projectors make the finished theme visible to all in the class.
Its merits and defects are judged by classmates, not by the teacher,—who
steps down from the status of Lord High Executioner to act as a permissive
group leader.

If a student's theme tells the reader clearly and economically how to clean
ignition points, so that anyone can follow the instructions, it is good communication, regardless of spelling or grammar. This is the kind of writing,
furthermore, which most students will do throughout their lives. Only a few
will ever be professional authors. Meanwhile, students writing themes for
classmates soon feel the need to get spelling and grammar under control.

Semantics is another technique of agreement. It is a study, as you know,
of human communication. It helps to understand both other people and ourselves better than we ever did before. I have been at it for 15 or 16 years and
I can testify that it works. On my desk is a motto sent me by Beardsley Ruml
which reads: "reasonable men always agree if they understand what they are
talking about."

With a good grip on semantics, one is never taken in by verbal hocus pocus and guilt by association. It has been said and said truly that semantics is the demagog's worst friend. Take for instance the case of Senator Taft. Senator Taft once introduced a bill for public housing. Therefore, Senator Taft is a Communist. We laugh, but Senator Taft did not laugh. The real estate lobby would not have used it unless they knew that there were millons of people who would be taken in by it. Really we ought to call it guilt by verbal association, not guilt by physical association. For instance, a person who is seen often in the company of a second story man—well, it's a good idea to lock the windows when he is around. This, of course, is not just association through words.

However, people and organizations have a great many characteristics. The trick is to find one characteristic which both people (or organizations) have. For example, both Senator Taft and Communist Russia are interested in public housing—therefore, you leap to the conclusion that all characteristics are interchangeable. Another example—my grocer has cheated me and my grocer is a Yankee, therefore, all Yankees are cheats. The Communists are against Chiang Kai Chek—the State Department is dubious about Chiang Kai Chek—therefore, the State Department is run by Communists.

It is possible to prove anything about anyone by using this line of reason. I can prove that anyone of you is a Communist, or a Catholic, or anything you please, due to this false idea of guilt by verbal association.

Again, Semantics enables us to make the important distinction between fact and inference or value judgment. For example: this train is going at 20 miles an hour—that is a fact. It is late, we won't get to Chicago until it is too late —that is an inference from fact. It is a lousy railroad—it is never on time— that is the conclusion reached. Again and again when somebody asks about something we say it is a "hell of a thing." Semantics helps us to break up phony conflicts due to failure of meaning. So many of our worries and conflicts are due to a little man who isn't there.

III

A final case in group dynamics: During the shortages of World War II, the government wanted to educate housewives to buy cheaper cuts of meat. Alexander Bavelas, social science researcher, was asked to find the best way to get housewives to change deeply grooved habits.

He set up two structures and measured results from both. In the first, housewives, like college students, were given the standard lecture system.

In the second, housewives met in groups with a competent discussion leader and talked over the war, the food shortage, balanced diets, vitamins, and various cuts of meat. As a result, *over ten times* as many women changed their buying habits as with the first system! The lectures told the women what to do and most of them balked. Practicing group dynamics they told *themselves* what to do and ten times as many began to act.

As I compiled the inventory, five general principles kept cropping up, like recurring decimals. Agreement is aided and conflict reduced by:

1. The principle of participation. The more persons actively involved in a given decision, the better it is likely to stick.

2. The principle of *cooperative action*. We release our inhibitions and expand our personalities through appropriate group action. A good group makes us a better adjusted individual. Hermits and recluses are abnormal.

3. The principle of *clearing communication lines*. "Reasonable men always agree if they understand what they are talking about." So many of our rows are due to little men who are not there, creatures of semantic confusion.

4. The principle of *facts first*. When sides begin to form and emotions mount, get in more facts. They will often indicate a basis of agreement which both sides can accept.

5. The principles of a *feeling of security*. A secure person is not nearly so ready to start a fight. We could use this principle to stop the spread of Communism, which thrives on insecurity, by pushing our Point 4 programs more forcefully.

IV

To strengthen the philosophy of cooperatives, we must put renewed emphasis on man as a social animal. The three facts I have mentioned are very pertinent to your own philosophy. You are on the right track scientifically, there is no question about it; and this work in human relations should be just your meat. It can strengthen your production and specific techniques and improve your publicity, or your contacts not only with the public but inside your own groups with your own members. If you operate a factory or a petroleum refinery they are all pertinent. They can improve your cooperative meetings, show you how to deal with management problems and leadership problems; also, they can be very helpful in relations with international organizations.

I remember Mary Arnold back in the old days at the cooperative conferences, how insistent she was about learning new techniques in accounting. I was practicing accounting then. We came up with a series of invaluable techniques in over-all relations, perhaps even more valuable than the last word in accounting. I speak as a CPA. Yes, there are many details, many techniques that help us improve our human relations, more than I ever imagined when I began this survey and now I feel much more optimistic. Meanwhile, our jobs become more challenging and the world situation seems less ominous as real progress is being made. But we can hardly rest on our oars.

FIVE GREAT AMERICANS

By *Paul H. Douglas*

This speech says far more than is found in the mere words themselves. To know what it really says, one must go back to the events and mood of the year 1951. That was the year of political denunciation and counterdenunciation over the dismissal of Douglas

MacArthur as Far Eastern commander. It was the year the Kefauver Committee disclosed alliance between politicians, police, and racketeers. It was the year the Fulbright Committee found political influence in making Reconstruction Finance Corporation loans. It was the year the McCarran Committee on Internal Security uncovered Communist apparatus and disloyalties. It was the year the King Committee found irregularities in the Bureau of Internal Revenue. It was a year loud with the shrill voices of men who saw only good in their own cause, or party, and dishonesty if not treason in the other man's.

In the midst of clamor Senator Douglas chose a theme on which all Americans could unite. Not in the speech itself, but in its overtones, he is saying: "Let us stop name-calling long enough to remember that America has a heritage of great men and women, and of great deeds." Perhaps also he was saying: "Public corruption recently come to light is only transient; fundamentally we are a great nation." So it was that he departed from his usual speaking mode ,of fact-filled and closely-knit arguments, and used instead timely illustrations and obvious references to current events.

The speech was given on the American Broadcasting Company network, August 12, 1951. The speaker was formerly professor of industrial relations in the University of Chicago, a private and then a major in the Marine Corps during World War II who had been wounded and awarded the Bronze Star for heroic service. When the speech was given he was a United States Senator from Illinois.

IN THESE DAYS of denunciations and counterdenunciations, I thought it might be well tonight to speak about five Americans, who are in danger of being forgotten but who by their work and lives have helped to make us all better men and women.

I

The first is John Woolman, the Quaker tailor who was born early in the eighteenth century, lived a life of apparent obscurity but who was the spiritual fountainhead of the antislavery movement in America. Slowly it dawned on Woolman as a young man that slavery was a great moral wrong. Human beings were treated as property and frequently overworked and cruelly handled. The system brutalized both the slave and the master. But it was widespread and it was profitable. Almost no one questioned it and most men of means owned slaves. But Woolman's inner voice would not let him rest. It told him slavery was wrong and that he should bear testimony against it. So he quietly traveled over the country speaking at Quaker meetings and to individual Quakers, urging them to stand out against slavery.

One by one, the Quaker yearly meetings passed resolutions asking all their members to free their slaves. Woolman was then given one of the most disagreeable jobs a man could have. He was appointed to a visiting committee to call on Quaker slaveholders and get them to free their bondsmen. He did this for years with such gentleness and humility that few harsh words were ever spoken to him and by 1775 the Quakers had freed their slaves without a cent of compensation and were out from underneath the great curse of slavery. Freed from the profits of this institution, they furnished in the next three-quarters of a century the spiritual shock troops of the antislavery movement.

How much better it would have been had others followed the example of Woolman and his associates! Had this been done, we need never have had the Civil War with all of its terrible loss of life, and the relations between the races and the sections would today be infinitely more friendly. But because the people would not follow John Woolman and the way of love, they had to take John Brown and the way of force, with Grant to boot.

II

The second man I want to speak about was a black-bearded German immigrant who fought in the Civil War, came to Chicago, practiced law, and in 1892 became Governor of Illinois. His name was John Peter Altgeld. At a time when women worked twelve hours a day or more in factories, he helped pass an 8-hour law—the first of its kind in this country. Resentful of injustice, he pardoned a group of anarchists who had been convicted of murder in connection with the Haymarket riots. He did this not because he sympathized with their aims, which he did not, but because he believed with reason that they had not received a fair trial and that there was no adequate evidence to indicate their guilt. But perhaps his noblest act was at the completion of his term. He had been beaten for reelection and he had lost his fortune. At this very juncture, Charles T. Yerkes, the corrupt streetcar magnate, was getting from the Illinois Legislature a fifty-year franchise for the use of Chicago's streets without compensation. Yerkes went to Altgeld, offered him $500,000 in currency which was in a safety deposit box in Chicago, if he would allow the bill to become law without his signature. Altgeld was sorely tempted. He took the key to the box, counted the money, found it was not marked, and then took counsel with his conscience. At the eleventh hour, he returned the key to Yerkes and vetoed the traction bill with a stinging message which concluded, "I cannot sell out the people of Chicago." Then, his term over, beaten and disgraced, and with only seven dollars in his pocket, he took the day coach to Chicago. The only man who met him was Joe Martin, the former gambler who loved Altgeld with all his heart and who had a keener insight into true virtue than most of the self-righteous people.

It was of Altgeld that our prairie poet, Vachel Lindsay, wrote:

> Sleep on, Eagle forgotten,
> Under the stone,
> Time has its way with you
> And death has its own.

But Lindsay continued: "To live in mankind, is far, far more than to live in a name."

The tenderness and the integrity of John Peter Altgeld lives on in the people of my state of Illinois and elsewhere.

III

The third person was Jane Addams, the miller's daughter, who started Hull House in the slums of Chicago in 1889 and who for nearly fifty years fed the hungry, clothed the naked, and cared for the sick in body and soul. Nor did she stop there. Miss Addams and her associates opened the first playground, established day nurseries, started the Juvenile Protective Association and the juvenile court, took care of immigrants, got the garbage out of the streets and alleys and helped with protective legislation for women and children.

Believing that the poor should have beauty as well as bread, she sponsored dance classes and a little theater, organized a music and an art school and developed an industrial museum which preceded the great museums of Munich and Chicago. Out of her insight into the hungers of the human heart, Jane Addams became one of our most penetrating and poignant writers. Her books such as *Twenty Years at Hull House, Democracy and Social Ethics, New Ideals of Peace, The Spirit of Youth,* and *The City Streets* and *The Devil-Baby at Hull House* are part of the permanent classics of our literature. A devoted worker for peace and international understanding, Jane Addams went further than most of us would go but she sowed on a wide scale the seeds of active good will.

A citizen of the world, she was also firmly rooted in Halsted Street and the Bloody Twentieth Ward of Chicago. She combined both character and culture to a rare degree and after knowing her for many years, I would say she was one of the two authentic saints whom I have ever met.

IV

My fourth and fifth selections were both United States Senators. Namely, Robert M. La Follette, of Wisconsin, and his friend and fellow fighter George W. Norris, of Nebraska. La Follette, early in his career, had to decide whether or not he should make public an attempt to influence improperly the Supreme Court of his state. He decided to do so and was immediately attacked on the ground that he had betrayed a confidence. After several defeats, he was finally elected Governor of Wisconsin in 1900. Here he pushed through numerous reforms such as the establishment of a state income tax, the regulation of private utilities based upon a physical valuation of their property, a reform of the general property tax, the building up of the State University into one of the great free institutions of the land. a workmen's compensation act for industrial accidents and a host of other reforms.

One of these reforms was to establish a genuine system of civil service for state employees. This was fifty years ago; so that Wisconsin ranks with Massachusetts and New York as one of the pioneers in this movement. A problem which always comes up when civil service is first put into effect is what to do with the existing employees who were originally appointed on political grounds. Should they be turned out or retained? If they are of his own party or group, a governor generally tends to blanket them in as permanent civil servants and thus try to give them permanent jobs. If the employees belong to the opposition, however, it is a common practice for a governor to oust them, replace them with his own men and then put these under the protection of civil service.

But this tends to poison the system from the very start. For when the opposition takes power, they cannot be expected to abide by the results. The new regime will therefore get rid of those who have the jobs on one pretext or another and give the positions to their own followers. Under these conditions, a true merit system becomes impossible and civil service a more or less hypocritical farce.

When La Follette became governor. his enemies manned the state jobs and he must have been sorely tempted. But he refused to fire his opponents and instead gave them civil-service tenure. No one could legitimately doubt his sincerity after that and as a result the merit system has probably been developed more fully in Wisconsin than in any other state. For that full credit should be given to Robert M. La Follette.

La Follette was then elected to the Senate and immediately started out on a vigorous program to preserve competition and prevent monopoly. When he first rose to speak in the Senate, all his Republican colleagues left the Chamber but the time came when not only the whole Senate but the whole country listened when he spoke. He passed a law to protect seamen and worked constantly for a proper physical valuation of the railroads to squeeze the "water" out of their capitalization. His son, Robert M. La Follette, Jr., who succeeded him, served for twenty years more and by his skill and fairness won the title of "Senators' Senator."

V

George W. Norris was a Nebraska lawyer who came to Congress in 1902 and found it dominated by big business. The House of Representatives was then ruled by Speaker Cannon who in effect appointed all committees and decided which Congressman should be permitted to speak and which bills could be called up for action. Norris stood this as long as he could and then with a few other Progressive Republicans joined the Democrats to replace the absolute monarchy of the Speaker with what has turned out to be the tempered autocracy of the Rules Committee.

Coming to the Senate in 1912, Norris served in that body for thirty years. He was active in every good cause, but his two greatest works were, first in getting the so-called anti-lame duck amendment passed which made Congress more responsive to the popular will and secondly, in creating, with Franklin Roosevelt's help, the Tennessee Valley Authority, which has done so much to build up that area. A hard-boiled and cynical politician once told me of Norris, "You can't buy him, nor flatter him nor frighten him. He always does what he thinks is right." And then wistfully with tears running down his face, he said, "I wish I could be like George Norris." And I would add that many of us believe he was the finest and purest senator of the last century.

In these days of strain and turmoil, we can take strength in the examples of John Woolman, John Peter Altgeld, Jane Addams, Bob La Follette and George Norris, who served the people of this nation. They were bitterly attacked and criticized in their day, but their lives have stood the test of time.

In the words of George Eliot, they have joined "the choir invisible of those immortal dead, who live in minds made better by their presence." But at times one hopes that mankind can recognize such men and women while they are living and not merely after they have died. I shall close, therefore, with the final words of Bernard Shaw in his play, *Saint Joan*: "O God that madest this beautiful earth, when will it be ready to receive Thy saints. How long, O Lord, how long?"

TO MAXIMIZE ONE'S LIFE

By *Cornelia Otis Skinner*

THIS ADDRESS was given at the Commencement of Mills College, Oakland, California, June 4, 1950. The speaker is an actress, an author, and a woman. You will note how deeply she draws upon the experience of all three for her ideas and her supporting materials, so much so that if one read the speech without knowing the speaker's name the reactions would be: "This is a woman, with a woman's sense of values," and almost as soon, "She is an actress who has lived through the deep tension that comes before the opening night," and finally, "From her knowledge of literature, she must be either a writer or critic."

I DOUBT IF any young woman of this University ever approached a tough assignment with more trepidation than this not-so-young woman is experiencing over this assignment. For a commencement address *is* a tough assignment for the most experienced of speakers. But when the speaker is not experienced, when she is not even a speaker, you can, if you'll put yourselves in her quaking shoes, imagine her state of mind. I find myself experiencing the familiar panic of that recurrent nightmare peculiar to actors in which a ghoulish bevy of directors and fellow players are bustling one onto a strange stage shouting "Hurry! Hurry! You're late!" And one has no idea of what one's part is, or for that matter what the play is: And one arrives before the audience completely speechless and, often as not, completely naked. Things are not quite that crucial for I do seem able to speak and I do appear to be clad. . . . And in this impressive costume with which your costume department has so kindly furnished me. Forgive such theatrical terminology, but an academic gown for me *is* a costume and a contributing factor to my platform fright is the realization that I have little right to wear it. For I never graduated from any college . . . and that toughens the toughness of the assignment.

I've been trying to brace myself up by recalling the fact that in my day . . . that day on which I did not graduate . . . students didn't listen any too attentively to commencement addresses. But this is a different type of day and students, thank heavens, are a very different type of student . . . which in a sense, is a different type of comfort.

I

What on earth can an ordinary, academically half-baked actress say to a group of (I'm sure) extraordinary graduates, baked to a turn and fresh from the ovens of learning? What does anyone say on these occasions? It is a temptation to fall back on the commencement day cliches, those observations about the threshold of life and the conventional congratulations to the generation "Who are About to go Forth Into the World." And then, one gives a sober thought to that world and wonders if any member of this generation is to be congratulated upon being "About to go Forth Into It." Certainly the generations that went forth ahead of you haven't made it much of a world for you. As a member of one of those preceding generations, I feel very humble, very apologetic. I feel that it is you who should be addressing us. Although it would probably do no good, as an older generation is an unregenerate one, too set in its ways and mistakes for redemption. You'd be wasting your energy. And you must not waste an ounce . . . or is it an *erg* of that energy . . . especially now while it is fresh and unjaded and you are still aware of how it should be expended. That energy can so easily and so quickly become mechanical or forced, and all too many of us eventually let it peter out, as being not worth the effort.

It is so easy for an older person to hand out advice which one hasn't taken oneself . . . so easy to say what not to be and what not to do. And so difficult to say what to be and how to go about being it. I can offer no practical procedure. I can only offer a suggestion, a suggestion that for a moment you project yourselves forward to what to you will seem an astronomically distant date . . . the date of your 25th reunion. To this undoubtedly each of you will come flocking with enthusiasm, a few minor infirmities and perhaps a fifteen-year-old daughter whom you're entering here and who, although she loves you dearly is quite mortified by you most of the time. It takes a certain brash courage to admit that my class at college (that class with which I did not graduate) recently held its 25th reunion. I was unable to attend it, but I listened with keen interest to a friend's description of our former classmates and of the persons they had become after twenty-five years.

No need for me to cite the examples as awful warnings. There was the person like the character in the play *Craig's Wife* whose house and its keeping had become a psychotic obsession . . . to whom an overturned ashtray on the carpet appeared more disastrous than an overthrown government in Europe. There was the high-pressure career girl, smartly "up" on "things" . . . such as psycho-analysis, canasta, the gown collection of Christian Dior and the poetry collection of T. S. Eliot. There was that suburban goddess of fertility, the professional mother, a wealth of gratuitous information regarding P.T.A., headmasters of prep schools, diapers, child psychology and prizes for flower arrangements. There was that tragic figure . . . the former glamor girl . . . "Prom Trotter" she was called in my day of blonde-preferring gentlemen . . . grown raddled and haggard in hysterical attempts to cling onto a youth which she really never had . . . still trying to look like Mary Miles Winger. There was that awesome female, the great American Club Woman, whose hand, frustrated at rocking the cradle finds strident outlet in knocking the gavel. There was the ultra-precious highbrow, whose rarefied mind was an enamel treasure-casket of gems of exquisitely rare information, secure in her ivory tower . . . quite unaware that ivory towers are part of the rubble of our times. There was the successful wife of the successful business man, expert at giving the right parties for the right people, the staunch patron of fashionable doctors who give her fashionable shots of fashionable vitamins. You know these types . . . these stereotypes . . . too busy being busy to live. Or, as Yeats put it, "So busy whether at work or play that all is forgotten but the momentary air." You have seen them among the older generation, you can see them in embryo among your own.

But fortunately you can see also another sort of person . . . the woman who has not constricted herself to being a type . . . who belongs to no generation because she is quite ageless. She is younger now than she was 25 years ago, than you are today . . . for her growing up has been a growing young, her maturity a process of renaissance, a mental and spiritual growth, nurtured by perception and awareness. She is that enviable person who, to borrow the words of Lord Tweedsmuir in regard to Arthur Balfour . . . who knows "How to maximize life." To maximize one's life . . . that's rather a wonderful phrase . . . the sort of phrase one could wish would catch in one's subconscious instead of the usual crazy jingles or those tunes that go "round and round." *To Maximize One's Life* strikes me as being one of the best objectives we might set ourselves. It is a highly individual objective and we must each go about its attainment according to our individual lights, and I need not point out, that those lights radiate from the inner and individual vision.

II

Each of us at some time has known that inner and individual vision. Each of us has had the choice of whether to keep that vision clear and alive or whether to let it fade and vanish. Perhaps man's most wonderful and terrible responsibility is the responsibility of vision and choice. To make the choice of pursuing that vision and to maintain that pursuit is no easy matter. At times it seems to take on the hopeless unreality of the pursuit of a mirage. And yet that mirage is probably our only reality in these horrifying times when the splitting atom has disproved the surety of matter or the continuation of life. A good nebulous vision would surely be a much snugger refuge than the super-fortified bomb shelter of Colonel McCormick. It is about the only thing on which we can count in this sorry world . . . and if more people counted on it, the world would be a lot less sorry. We can't count on present day civilization. It would be comforting to believe that we might count on our fellow man. But man under the brutal exigencies of the times can be sadly lacking in fellowship. Some of you, and you are indeed fortunate, can count on the solaces of an accepted religion, but faith in a conventionally established faith can wobble and some times vanish for good . . . and what is there to take its place? There is the vision . . . and our choice to follow it. And maybe that isn't too bad a religion in itself.

For the vision is always there. It is fleeting, to be sure, as fleeting as the shimmering maiden described by William Blake. Its aspect is forever changing. It must change as our perceptions change, as experience shifts and refines our awarenesses. And the irony of dedicating ourselves to the pursuit of this vision is that we never do attain it . . . which is the divine irritant, that goads us into constant observation, that makes life possible.

This vision of our private ideal, this lighting-flash picture of our innate endowments creates the same impact which stirs and goads the artist. Perhaps it should be spoken of purely in terms of art; because living is the greatest of the arts and all artists are not to be found purely within the confines of the plastic, the fine or the liberal arts. For all the number of the future distinguished among you . . . the painters, actresses, musicians, writers to be, there will also be a number of the quite undistinguished, whose occupation the next census will list as mere "housewife," but who in their way are true artists. They have chosen the way of awareness, the way of the vision, the way of the artist.

It takes courage to make that choice and to continue in it, for the way of the artist is hard . . . filled with disappointment, with more heartbreak than reward, more discipline than delight. The outcome of the original compulsion can so easily fall into apathy, particularly if one depends for its continuance upon that nebulous prospect, the recurrent moments of inspiration. You know as well as I do that inspiration is not to be counted upon. It comes through no voluntary summons. It comes, when it comes at all, of its own accord, often after days, weeks, months of plugging work, of technical labor. Every pursuer of art must enter his or her own relentless school of technique. It is an exacting school which grants no holidays but continues always until death hands out the diplomas. In it one acquires the hard education of self-searching, education in the courage to be constantly taking apart and reassembling, to be constantly perfecting even when knowing that perfection will never be reached. The sort of courage which prompted Renoir when he was well in his forties to go back to elementary art class in order to improve his drawing . . . or the French actor Talbot at the age of 80 to ask the critic Paul Menter to come see his performance of *L'Avare* . . . a part he must have played a thousand times: "Come see me play *L'Avare*," he wrote "Je fais des progres . . . I'm improving." Paradoxically that sort of searching of the self is the only way in which we succeed in losing the self. This inexorable school is a sort of never ceasing production line from which the true artist can never take time off to be impressed by the results of production. To be impressed or depressed by results is the easiest of distractions. There are many distractions. Public opinion is the strongest, dangerous when it's over favorable, brutal when it is not, when we have the bitter experience of realizing that people fail to understand what we are trying to convey. That opinion which to be sure can at times be helpful, must never for an instant swerve us from what we know in our hearts we *are* trying to convey. For honesty is the great requisite of art. If we remain honest with ourselves, art, which is always there, never lets us down. We can only let ourselves down. And when we do, we let ourselves into our own individual hell. In this distressing regional connection, let me read you these somewhat terrifying words spoken by Gian-Carlo Menotti at a town hall lecture last March:

> Hell begins on the day when God grants us a clear vision of all that we might have achieved, of all the gifts which we have wasted, of all that we might have done which we did not do.

> The poet shall forever scream the poems which he never wrote; the painter will be forever obsessed by visions of the pictures which he did not paint; the musician will strive in vain to remember the sounds which he failed to set down on paper.

> There are few artists whom I can imagine resting in heavenly peace: Leonardo, Michelangelo, Goethe, and a few minor artists who have merited that peace. But for the weak, the lazy, the damned—their torture shall be the more horrible in pro portion to the greatness of the genius they have wasted.

> For me the conception of Hell lies in two words: *Too late*.

III

Well, for you, it is anything but "too late." Each of you today has received the impressively engraved skin of a dead sheep, which, according to popular opinion indicates that you have also received an education. And that is certainly one of our bigger and better fallacies, because surely each young woman graduating today must be excitingly aware that her education is only just beginning. Her higher education is her own individual university of which she is dean, president, student body and janitor. You who are about to go forth into the world . . . there! I knew that cliché would come out sooner or later. Well, you *are* going forth into the world. And it's not a pretty world. It's a world of dreadful uncertainty. But that very uncertainty of the world can give you your own certainties. And when it does, you will know them for your certainties. They will be clear and simple. They may even seem prosaic. But I beg of you to keep them so . . . to have the courage of your platitudes. Because life is simple. The vision is simple and to follow it is our certainty. You will know times of misgiving, you may in yourselves never find complete security but you can always find courage . . . the courage to live by your lights, the courage to maximize your lives.

Elie Faure has said that "art is the appeal to the instinct of communion in men." Each of you is a potential artist who by making life an art will make it better for yourself and so better for your fellow man. To make it so, you will need your certainties, which are all you can count upon . . . your honesty, your integrity, your courage and . . . your vision. God speed you one and all.

OUR ISSUE WITH RUSSIA

By *T. V. Smith*

THIS SPEECH has three especially distinguished qualities. First, its analysis of the issue between the U.S.A. and the U.S.S.R. is more penetrating than in other good speeches. It goes beneath the superficial surface differences, down to the ultimate issue itself. You will note that such an analysis would be impossible without an intimate knowledge of American history.

Second, this analysis is set forth in three main heads, each of them phrased tersely, unmistakably, and almost unforgettably.

Third, the quality of supporting material is rare even among good speeches, not only because it is skillfully used but also because of its variety. You will find in it each of the nine forms of support discussed in Chapter 7.

The speech was given before the 11th General Assembly of the States, in Chicago, December 5, 1952. The speaker was formerly a state senator and a United States Congressman, a magazine editor, a private in World War I and a colonel in World War II He is now professor of philosophy and politics in Syracuse University.

YOU HAVE been concerned primarily with problems, I note. I suppose that is proper grist for your mill, but I would much prefer to deal with our blessings, to celebrate our achievements both in legislation and in education, rather than to take too critical a point of view today. And, by way of giving you some perspective, let me begin with this quotation:

> It is a gloomy moment in history. Not for many years, not in the lifetime of most men who read this, has there been so much grave and deep apprehension. Never has the future seemed so incalculable as at this present hour.
>
> In France the political caldron seethes and bubbles with uncertainty. Russia hangs, as usual, a cloud dark and silent upon the horizon of Europe, while all the energies, resources and influences of the British Empire are sorely tried and are yet to be tried more sorely.
>
> It is a solemn moment, and no man can feel indifferent to the issue of events. . . . Of our own troubles here, no man can see the end.

From *Harper's Weekly*, 1857.

My Grandad, viewing earth's worn cogs, said things were going to the dogs.
His Grandad, in his house of logs, said things were going to the dogs.
And his Grandad, in the Flemish bogs, said things were going to the dogs.
There is one thing now that I want to state: the dogs have had a good long wait.

In connection with our problems—many of which either disappear or take on manageable proportions with the increasing perspective which history furnishes—there is one general situation, or climate of opinion, if you like, under which you will be tackling, no doubt, all of the problems which you do tackle; and this is a situation with which you are, I take it, as state legislators, not primarily concerned, but from which, God helping you, you will not be able to escape. It is with reference to that climate of opinion that I want to speak during these brief moments.

"Just in Case," I mean to say, that some state legislator might be tempted to try to manage the communistic problem at the state level, rather than leave it to Congress and the FBI, we ought to try in advance to reduce the risk, the real risk, that we may do more harm to our friends, through the method we use, than to our foes, by the results we achieve.

In this spirit of risk-reduction, after some experience with the problem at both levels, and internationally also, I hazard the impression, from long years of relation to politics and education, that the greatest weakness we Americans have in dealing with Communism is that we aren't, ourselves, quite converted to our own system, namely, American capitalism. We have not yet got deeply into our Christian souls, always prone to sympathy, that the harsher path of competition is the only form of cooperation in the world which can maintain itself among civilized men. In this confusion we are apt to play into the hands of the Russians, even to talk like them.

Note this remark, made by Marshal Zhukov to General Eisenhower, the General reporting it in the last chapter of that great book of his, *Crusade in Europe:*

> The Marshal seemed to be a firm believer in the Communist concept. He said that as he saw it, the Soviet system of government was based on idealism, and ours upon materialism. In expanding his idea of this difference, he remarked [and introduced an

apology for criticizing my country] that he felt our system appealed to all that was selfish in people. He said we induced a man to do things by telling him he might keep what he earned, might say what he pleased, and, in every direction, allowing him to be largely undisciplined, unoriented within a great national complex.

He asked me to understand the system on the other side, in which the attempt was made to substitute for such motivations a devotion of a man to the great national complex of which he formed a part.

Mr. Eisenhower goes on to say, "In spite of my complete repudiation of such contentions and my condemnation of all systems that involved dictatorship, there was no doubt," adds our General, now our President-elect, "that Marshal Zhukov was sincere."

Now, there are in America continuous attacks upon the profit system as somehow being selfish, upon the notion that men *shall* keep what they get and say what they please, and in every way act, as he put it, as individual units, "unoriented within a great national complex."

We are taught on Sunday, from most of our churches, that capitalism somehow is morally inferior and so is suspect. The great Roman Catholic Church has never engaged itself with the capitalistic system. It is opposed to, and recommends a substitute for, the capitalistic system. In the Protestant churches we are turning out ministers who, in the name of the brotherhood of man, weaken the notion in American life that competition is the most fruitful relationship between men, and make invidious distinction between what they call "human rights," and what from our Founding Fathers have been called "property rights."

We are subject to such idealistic attrition against the very nature of our system that I think we are due to get clear in our minds what it is we do believe, Sunday as well as Monday. It is time we realized that this system which we have—of private profit and of competition between men and between groups—even competition between religions—is the only thing which keeps virtue on the grow, and vice forever on the skids.

I propose, therefore, to put it very simply. What is the great issue between us and Communism that we must get clearly in mind if, in fighting them, we are not to do exactly what a general would do in letting the other general choose the battlefield on which battle is to be made? To be mixed up in our ideas about this, itself constitutes a surrender to the other side of the vast advantage. Clarity is the secret weapon of the cold war.

I suggest to you that there are three ways of formulating the fundamental issue between us and Communism.

The first is the notion that the issue is a religious difference. The second is the notion that it is an economic difference. Both of these—I ask you to let me suggest to you—must be disallowed as being, in themselves, fraught with danger for the American way of life. But, specifically, there are a good many millions of our fellow citizens, I do not doubt, who think that the fundamental issue between us and the Russians is a religious issue. That notion, I am convinced, will do us more harm than it does them. The Russians are an atheistic nation. On both party sides in the recent campaign you heard orators drag in the phrase, "Godless Russia." Well, Russia *is* godless. They have pride in being atheist. We, on the other side, are Christian, though the Supreme Court,

in formulating that, says that we are "also a nation with the duty to survive."
Men survive only that "unchristian" habit of competing with each other.
even in a pinch to the very death.

This is *an* issue. We are a Christian people, and they are not only unchristian but they are a godless people. I don't deny that this is important,
this difference. We set a great deal of stead on our being Christian. They set
a great deal of stead on their being atheistic. It is an important issue, but it
is not *the* issue; and we cannot conceivably afford to obscure our minds with
this false formulation of the issue.

I. RELIGION IS NOT "THE" ISSUE

It is not *the* issue, for a very simple reason; and that reason is the Constitution of the United States. We had so much experience before we formu-
lated the Constitution—of unchristian struggle between Christian churches,
in the name of which brothers were willing to liquidate each other—that when
we came to formulate our Constitution, we said that religion shall never be
made a test of citizenship in the United States, neither for voting nor office-
holding nor anything else. So we wrote into our great Bill of Rights, in the
very opening sentence, that not even Congress shall make any law as touch-
ing the establishment of religion, or prohibiting the free exercise thereof.

We must remember also that freedom *for* religion, in the Constitution,
also means freedom *from* religion. In other words we learned before this
Republic was founded that we cannot make religious matters a test of rights
or privileges.

This has often been brought home to my mind—what we have learned in
America—by my long-standing friendship with a distinguished son of this
great city, Clarence Darrow. Clarence Darrow, you know, was what passed
for an atheist. I will not speak technically of his agnosticism. Many who
knew Clarence Darrow thought him to be a Christ-like man in his conduct—
the most tolerant, I thought, the most charitable, the most merciful man, that
I myself had ever known.

I remember well. when I was home from Congress one time, he came up
to my office, his old, weather-beaten face just beaming with joy. I said,
"Clarence, you must have got word that some rich uncle died and left you
all his money. I never saw you look so happy."

He said, "I'm happy, all right. As much as I need money, this is better
than any legacy I could have got from a rich uncle."

I said, "Come on, old friend. Tell me what you have discovered."

He said, "I have discovered how to get rid of religion."

I said, "I know you have always been going around debating with
preachers and rabbis and priests, and the only effect I ever saw was that you
fell in love with every one of them that you have ever met."

He said, "That always bothered me as much as it did you. I knew there
was something wrong there, but I couldn't despise these people."

"Well, what have you discovered?" I asked.

He said, "I have discovered how to get rid of religion at last."

I said, "This is really something. Go on. Don't expect me to join you, but I'll hear you through."

He said, "Well, don't you remember in reading the biographies of all the great men that they got religion at their mother's knees?"

"Yes," I said. "So what?"

"Well, don't you see?" he said. "Just pass a law cutting off all mother's knees, and we can stop it at its source."

Now, the fact that Clarence Darrow was an agnostic—or even an atheist, if you could prove it so—was not something that I approved, or something that most of you approve; but the beauty of this Republic is that we learned before the Constitution was written that you can't drag religion into citizenship. The man who is an atheist has as much right, as an American citizen, as a man who isn't.

Now, having learned that magnificent lesson on how to get along with an atheist in the name of American citizenship, wouldn't we be in a leaky boat if we let religious sectarians drag us into a war with Russia because communists insist on being only what we admit that we have a right to be in the United States? No, religion is a false lead in trying to find the bottom issue with Russia.

II. PRIVATE PROPERTY IS NOT "THE" ISSUE

The second formulation comes from Russia, and is equally to be disallowed, I think; for reasons I shall give, very briefly. Is the test of citizenship economic in nature—whether or not property shall be privately owned?

Now, this is an issue between us. We hold to the system of private property, even if on Sunday we are shaky about private profit. The communists hold that you must not have any private property, though they have modified that is recent times to say "property of a certain sort," namely, the means of production.

Now, take that issue. Property is not the issue, either—though this will subject me to more criticism from you.

This is not conceivably the proper way of formulating the issue between us and Russia—that they believe in no private property generally and we believe in having as much private property as possible. The reason why we cannot make that the issue between us is the same reason as in the religious case. The reason is the Constitution of the United States.

Whether we like it or not, the Founding Fathers were so wise about this business that they did not build this Republic upon the notion that any amount of property of any kind has to be privately owned. It is true that they believed in private property, but they also believed in flexibility with reference to what property should be private and what should be public.

I think a great American of our generation has put the matter exactly right when he says,

Diversity and flexibility rather than the stereotyped hard-and-fast system is an essential part of such a noble concept of society as is ours.

We get our economic services in the way that, at the time, seems to work best, that will in a particular situation, best advance our underlying purposes.

We do not start with all the economic answers or the political answers. We make up the answers as we go along. Thus, American industry is owned and operated, by and large, by competitive private enterprise, yet . . . the Senate of the United States not long ago voted unanimously to establish public ownership and management in one of our largest industries, to make it a government monopoly. I refer to the atomic materials industry. That appeared to be the thing to do at the time, for reasons related to the facts of atomic energy, not for ideological reasons taken out of some book on economic dogma.

The most rock-ribbed midwestern town that I know of has, for many years, owned and operated its own electric power and light plant. Is this, then, a socialist town? Well, hardly. Its water service has been privately owned for the same period. There is a privately owned university and a public junior college there. No one considers that these things are inconsistent, and, of course, they are not, except to the dogmatist who thinks we have a fixed system.

In the same town I speak of there is a farmers' cooperative that is not quite private and not quite public, operating side by side with a big, non-profit insurance company. There are private banks, there are these non-profit insurance companies, there are state-owned liquor stores.

We would never consider adopting government ownership or control of newspapers, but our school system, the cornerstone of American education, is almost entirely publicly owned and publicly managed.

This is all a part of the familiar picture of American diversity, of American flexibility.

The truth is that we never did make a dogma in terms of which we can judge either political parties or citizens in these parties, as to how much property must be privately owned. We almost did.

In the decade before the Revolutionary War there were sold in the American Colonies as many copies of Blackstone's *Commentaries*—the great citadel of private property—as were sold in all of England at the time.

Blackstone says in the introduction to his *Commentaries,*—and I'm quoting —"So great is the regard of the [common] law for private property, that it will not authorize the least violation of it; no, not even for the general good of the whole community."

Now, that would make private property a dogma.

But our Revolution came at an opportune time to escape that dogma. So when Thomas Jefferson came to write the Declaration of Independence, and when we came to build the Constitution, instead of taking what then passed throughout the civilized world as being the proper ends of government— "life, liberty and property"—Jefferson wrote, "Life, liberty and *the pursuit of happiness.*" We know that he meant more than a rhetorical phrase, because a little later when he was our Minister in France, and when his old friend, Lafayette, came to him one night (as he ought not to have done to the American Minister) and showed to him the first draft of the French Declaration of the Rights of Man, he asked Jefferson to criticize it in the light of American experience. Jefferson took his pen and drew a line through one word, marking it out. They had "life, liberty and property." He cut off the word, "property," and left it "life, liberty" and a blank space.

Now, from that good day to this we had no dogma about what kind of property shall be owned and in what manner—whether publicly or privately. The Court has kept the Constitution as flexible on this point as it was made.

"That's what the shooting is mostly about. I mean the "shooting from the lip" in national campaigns—whether we shall move in the direction of having less and less privately owned property or more and more. That is an issue so deep and so open that, as a matter of fact, the parties have changed sides on this more than once, as to what direction we ought to go, but it always comes down to this fundamental fact: if we are going by the Constitution of the United States, we cannot make the dogma of private property any more than religious dogma the test of citizenship in the United States.

We have freedom of religion for everyone; we have freedom from religion for anyone.

Likewise for property. Each generation has the right to decide for itself, and that is the strength of this magnificent system, that property which has been privately owned may now be publicly owned, and property that has been publicly owned may now be privately owned. This is a legitimate source of controversy between us; and the variety of outcome constitutes the strength of the American economic system.

I submit, therefore, that these two ways of formulating the difference between us and Russia get our minds all fogged in such fashion that we are as likely to kill our friends as we are to hurt our enemies, if we go out armed in thought with these confusions.

III. "THE" ISSUE IS PROPERTY OF PRIVACY

I submit now, briefly, a third formulation which is *the real* issue between us and Russia. It is *not* the privacy of property; it *is* the property of human privacy. And note that remark well. When you change the venue from the privacy of property to the property of human privacy, you find an issue upon which we can stand firm and upon which we can fight with a determined and fixed resolve: to kill our enemies and to save our friends.

"But," you say, "the ownership of private opinion? Surely, nobody in the world would really want to own another man's soul." Well, that is something we really would not be able to believe if we hadn't had a lot of experience with it ourselves in another field. There is in man a will to power which feeds upon itself, and which can grow so pathological that it cannot content itself short of ownership of souls.

Let me just remind you of that experience. This is what led the founding fathers to keep religious dogma out of the Constitution—and out of American life.

When Roger Williams fled from that man of God, the Puritan John Cotton, to Rhode Island, calling that primitive outpost "Providence" because it saved his life from his own brothers in Massachusetts, he wrote a pamphlet to the British Parliament, entitled, "The Bloody Tenet of Persecution," in which he said, "These Puritans who came over here to get freedom for their conscience now drive me out of Massachusetts because I follow my conscience."

John Cotton replied to that with a pamphlet entitled, "The Bloody Tenet of Persecution Washed and Made White in the Blood of the Lamb," in which he said, "We didn't drive you out of Massachusetts, as you aver, because you followed your conscience. We drove you out because you refused to follow your conscience in doing what you well knew to be right." And he left it at that. And if that isn't clear, let me make it transparent.

As an illustration, a friend of mine who was then a Christian minister out on the South Side of Chicago, was visiting across the lake one day at what in those days was quite a show place, the "House of David." You will recall their long-haired baseball team. This House of David was a very prosperous cult that was built, among other things, on the proposition that if you would sell your property and give it to "King David" or "Queen Mary," you would never die. This is better than social security.

They went out to a lot of simple-minded farmers and other people in the United States who said, "That's a bargain in any man's language," and so bought immortality—until the cult became very wealthy.

Well, my friend was going through the place, being shown by a young guide. He called the guide off at the end of the tour and said, "I don't want to embarrass you before the rest of the people, but may I ask you a personal question? Tell me, what do you do with your members when they *do* die?"

This young fellow, quite unabashed, so deep was his faith, spoke up for everybody to hear. "What do we do with them when they do die? We turn them over to the undertaker, of course. The fact that they go off and die is a sure sign that they never did really belong to us in the first place." Well, I see you got the point.

John Cotton said, "We didn't persecute you for your conscience; we persecuted you because you refused to follow your conscience." He was making a dogma of his religious beliefs and insisting on his ownership of Williams' conscience: *You haven't any conscience unless you have mine.* I'll load yours with the beliefs it requires to be like mine. Now, generalize this attitude, from religion where we have known it, to economics, politics, art and science; and you will have the Russian insistence upon Party property in all privacy.

They have always insisted upon party ownership of private beliefs about politics, about economics, and about religion. But of late they have invaded the private field of art—and now at last the field of science. So that there is no longer any doubt whatsoever that what they intend is the ownership of all private judgment whatsoever.

It is a fact that at last the Commissar of Art called the poets and the playwrights and the novelists together and said, in substance: "What is all this nonsense you've been writing in your poetry, novels and fiction? You can't do that. If you're going to write fine art products, you write them according to the specifications that we hand down from the Politbureau. We don't want to hear any more of this other stuff. I'll put into your minds the thoughts that you must have. I must own your souls, not you."

Well, that was pretty hard, but a lot of Americans still didn't wake up to it until two years or so ago Russia called a scientific conference, and, in the course of it, one man, largely unknown even in Russia—Lysenkof, by name—kept taking a large part in the proceedings. He was a geneticist, and he was so conspicuous that finally, after the discussion had gone on for a day or two, one of the remaining men of science asked him whether he was speaking for himself or for the regime.

He modestly admitted that he was speaking for the regime. Then those who didn't crawl on their stomachs to admit "error" and to make apologies, disappeared overnight, as the artists had done before them. Now, it is a scientific truth, by fiat, that men can and do inherit "acquired characteristics," whether they *do* or not. The party at last owns the souls of all members, and will put its own beliefs into every consciousness—and into every conscience.

We see now why they drive against the private ownership of property. It is in order to destroy the last defense men have for their own privacy. Destroy that moat to protect the soul in its citadel, and the soul is without defenses of its sacred privacy. We can now see, too, what it is that we have to object against their religious attitude and their suspicion of our private property. It is not that they insist upon being atheists. That is their right. It is that they insist that, we cannot be theists. And that insistence is our wrong. It is not that they attack the privacy of property. That is their right. It is that they will not, let us have private property. Their trouble is not their beliefs or their doubts. The trouble with them is that they make of their beliefs and their disbeliefs *dogmas* which deprive us of our rights to believe or not to believe.

It is dogma that does the damage; for the final debt of dogma is ownership of souls, so that the dogmatic beliefs may fully possess the private souls of men. This is the property of privacy, *the* final issue between us and communism.

We would defend a system in which, whatever the property rights may be, they do not reach to the privacy of men. We defend a system in which our great philosopher—Alfred North Whitehead—declares that "religion is what a man does with his solitariness." We defend a system in which our great jurist—Louis Brandeis—declares that the most precious right of civilized men is "the right to be let alone." We defend a system in which our greatest poet—Emily Dickinson—states the soul's royal supremacy:

> The soul selects her own society,
> Then shuts the door;
> On her divine majority
> Obtrude no more.

Having made at the Constitutional prime the greatest of all discoveries—namely, that men do not have to agree upon their fundamental beliefs, economic, political, or religious—in order to build a cooperative society (in fact realizing that they can build a stronger cooperation by fostering conflicting beliefs and competitive ideologies), we consolidate our historic gains, with Mr. Justice Jackson, in this final faith: "If there is any fixed star in our constitutional constellation it is that no official, high or petty, can prescribe what shall be orthodox in politics, nationalism, religion, or other matters of opinion, or force citizens to confess by word or act their faith therein."

With this issue clear, we know for what we live—and we know for what, in a pinch, we shall gladly die. Death for that is life immortal, and life for that is doorway to gladsome death.

INDEX